The Kids' Guide to the 1996 SUMMER OLYMPICS

BY THE EDITORS OF
SPORTS ILLUSTRATED FOR KIDS

THE KIDS' GUIDE TO THE 1996 SUMMER OLYMPICS

The Kids' Guide to the 1996 Summer Olympics
SPORTS ILLUSTRATED FOR KIDS publication/May 1996

SPORTS ILLUSTRATED FOR KIDS and  are registered trademarks of Time Inc.

Cover and interior design by Pegi Goodman
Illustrations by Mark Herman
Map and puzzle illustrations by Dixon Rohr
Research by Alex Bhattacharji and Ben Kaplan
All rights reserved. Copyright © 1996 Time Inc.

No part of this book may be reproduced or transmitted in any form or by any means, electronic or mechanical, including photocopying, recording, or by any information storage and retrieval system, without permission in writing from the publisher.

For information, address: SPORTS ILLUSTRATED FOR KIDS

> If you purchased this book without a cover, you should be aware that it is stolen property. It was reported as "unsold and destroyed" to the publisher, and neither the author nor the publisher has received any payment for this "stripped" book.

ISBN 1-886-74911-6

The Kids' Guide to the 1996 Summer Olympics is published by SPORTS ILLUSTRATED FOR KIDS, a division of Time Inc. Its trademark is registered in the U.S. Patent and Trademark Office and in other countries. SPORTS ILLUSTRATED FOR KIDS, 1271 Avenue of the Americas, New York, NY 10020.

PRINTED IN THE UNITED STATES OF AMERICA

10 9 8 7 6 5 4 3 2 1

THE KIDS' GUIDE TO THE 1996 SUMMER OLYMPICS is a production of SPORTS ILLUSTRATED FOR KIDS Books: Cathrine Wolf, Editorial Director; Stephen Malley, (Project Editor); Margaret Sieck, Senior Editor; Jill Safro, Associate Editor; Sherie Holder, Assistant Editor

New Business Development: David Gitow, Director; Stuart Hotchkiss, Associate Director; Pete Shapiro, Assistant Director; Mary Warner McGrade, Fulfillment Director; Bob Fox, Jahn Sandklev, Development Managers; John Calvano, Operations Manager; Donna Miano-Ferrara, Production Manager; Associate Development Managers, Mike Holahan, Allison Weiss; Dawn Weland, Assistant Development Manager; Charlotte Siddiqui, Marketing Assistant

PHOTO CREDITS
Allsport: 53 (Al Bello); 75 (Nathan Bilow); 74 (Markus Boesch); 43 (Shaun Botterill); 4, 35, 49, 95 (Simon Bruty); 30 (Chris Cole); 42, 88 (Tony Duffy); 7 (John Gichigi); 39 (Mike Hewitt); 4, 67 (Richard Martin/Vandy stat); 63 (Clive Mason); 4 (Gray Mortimore); 81 Don Morley; 11 (D. Pensinger); 31 (Gary M. Prior); 4, 21, 22, 26, 29, 56, 63, 71, 81, 94 (Mike Powell); 37 (Tony Quinn); 36 (Ben Radford); 50 (Jamie Squire); 57 (Todd Warshaw); 28, 70, 68, 64.
Allsport/Hulton Deutsch: 85.
Allsport/Vandystat: 89.
AP/Wide World: 26, 31, 32, 58, 59, 65, 76, 86, 87.
Rhona Wise/USA Baseball: 9.
Robert Beck: 73.
UPI/Bettmann: 10, 16, 48, 51, 71, 84.
John Biever: 80.
Dave Black: 15, 19, 88, 89, 90, 91, 95.
Bongarts: 23, 24, 33.
Brown Brothers: 86.
Duomo: 6.
USA Field Hockey: 25.
Casey B. Gibson: 38.
Dan Helms: 52, 56.
Doug Hoke/USA Softball: 41.
I.O.C. Archives: 87.
Long Photography: 77.
Photo Kishimoto: 8.
Photo Run: 61.
Sports Illustrated: 62 (Jerry Cooke); 17 (John Iacono); 45 (Richard Mackson); 13 (John W. McDonough); 27 (Manny Millan); 55 (Peter Read Miller); 47, 79 (Ron Modra); 89, 90 (Neil Leifer); 14, 69, 72.
U.S.O.C: 87.
Front-cover photos: Bill Frakes/Sports Illustrated (Carl Lewis); Dave Black (Shannon Miller, Bruce Baumgarten); AP/Wide World (Fu Mingxia); John W. McDonough/Sports Illustrated (Scottie Pippen).
Back-cover photos: Sports Illustrated (Vitaly Scherbo); Mike Hewitt/Allsport (Gwen Torrence); Dave Black (Scott Shipley); Allsport (Sergei Bubka); Doug Hoke/USA Softball (Michele Smith).

Table of Contents

Basketball . . . . page 10

Gymnastics . . . . page 26

Track and Field . . . . page 60

On the Cover: Carl Lewis, U.S. (large photo); (clockwise from top right): Fu Mingxia, China; Shannon Miller, U.S.; Scottie Pippen, U.S.; Bruce Baumgartner, U.S.

INTRODUCTION	4
ARCHERY	6
BADMINTON	7
BASEBALL	8
BASKETBALL	10
BOXING	16
CANOE/KAYAK	18
CYCLING	20
MOUNTAIN BIKING	22
EQUESTRIAN	23
FENCING	24
FIELD HOCKEY	25
GYMNASTICS	26
RHYTHMIC GYMNASTICS	31
JUDO	32
MODERN PENTATHLON	33
ROWING	34
SOCCER	36
SHOOTING	38
TEAM HANDBALL	39
SOFTBALL	40
SWIMMING	42
SYNCHRONIZED SWIMMING	52
WATER POLO	53
DIVING	54
TABLE TENNIS	57
TENNIS	58
TRACK AND FIELD	60
VOLLEYBALL	72
BEACH VOLLEYBALL	74
YACHTING	75
WEIGHTLIFTING	76
WRESTLING	78
WHAT DO YOU KNOW?	81
WELCOME TO ATLANTA	82
MOMENTS TO REMEMBER	84
SIMPLY AMAZING	86
WHATIZIT? AND OTHER QUESTIONS	88
THE WORLD OF THE SUMMER OLYMPICS	90
PUZZLES	92
SCHEDULE	94
ANSWERS	96

Introduction

Get ready for the world's biggest birthday party! The modern Olympics are 100 years old this year and the celebration is going to be amazing.

On July 19, a torch that was carried across the U.S. by 10,000 people will light a flame at Olympic Stadium, in Atlanta, Georgia. For the following 16 days, 10,700 athletes from 197 countries will compete in 26 sports. More than 2 million people will attend the Games, and more than 3 billion people will watch on TV. The 1996 Summer Olympics will be the biggest sports event ever held.

The Greeks created the Olympics more than 2,000 years ago. Every four years, during the summer, Greek athletes met in a spirit of friendship and peace. The Olympics were considered so important that wars stopped during the Games.

The lighting of the Olympic flame means the Games have begun.

These ancient Olympics ended in A.D. 394. The Games were revived in 1896 by Baron Pierre de Coubertin of France. In the first modern Olympics, 311 athletes from 13 countries competed.

The Olympics have been held every four years since, except 1916, 1940, and 1944, when world wars were being fought.

Countries have often refused to attend the Olympics for political reasons. But in 1996, for the first time in history, every country invited to the Olympics is expected to show up.

Some countries are new. At the 1992 Summer Olympics, a Unified Team competed. The team's athletes came from some of the 12 countries, called republics, that had made up the Soviet Union. The Soviet Union was dismantled in 1991. This year, those athletes will compete for their own republics, such as Russia, Ukraine, or Belarus. In addition, the former Czechoslovakia has split into two new countries: the Czech Republic and Slovakia.

This will be the fourth time the Summer Games have been held in the United States. (The most recent time was 1984, in Los Angeles, California.)

Hosting a party for the world isn't easy. Many of the citizens of Atlanta have been working for five years to prepare. Here are a few of the things that had to be done: building the Olympic Stadium

An archer lit the flame in 1992 in Barcelona.

The Olympics turn 100 years old this summer, and Atlanta is throwing a huge party to celebrate.

and seven new arenas; printing and selling 11 million tickets; building an Olympic village with rooms for more than 14,000 athletes, coaches, and team officials.

Still, there are going to be trouble spots. Finding places to stay for millions of fans and 15,000 reporters is a problem. More than 5,500 buses and cars are ready, but traveling even a few miles could take more than two hours. And it's going to be hot. Temperatures in Atlanta usually reach 90 degrees or higher every day in the summer. This will be tough for athletes and fans alike. More than 100 medical-aid stations have to be set up.

Georgia is not the only place to find the party. Soccer games will be played in Alabama (Birmingham); Florida (Miami and Orlando); and Washington, D.C. White-water canoe and kayak races will be held in Tennessee.

This book is your guide to all the excitement. You'll learn about the 26 Olympic sports, including the new ones: beach volleyball, mountain biking, and softball. You can read about the stars to watch and the athletes who became legends at past Olympics.

The 1996 Summer Olympics, in Atlanta, promise to be the biggest and best ever. And when the Games are over and the torch is put out, there won't be much time to rest. The 1998 Winter Olympics in Nagano, Japan, are less than two years away.

Let the games begin!

The flame theme reaches from torch relays to hot costumes.

Archery

At the opening ceremony of the 1992 Olympics, archer Antonio Rebollo of Spain lit the Olympic flame by shooting a flaming arrow into the air. Antonio's arrow only had to pass within six feet of the torch to light it.

To win a medal at the 1996 Olympics, an archer needs to be much more accurate than *that*.

Olympic archers will shoot at round targets 70 meters (230 feet) away. In the center of each target is a round, 4.8-inch bull's-eye, also called the gold ring. Surrounding the bull's-eye are nine rings, each 2.4 inches wide. Archers score 10 points for hitting the bull's-eye. The rings are worth from 9 points, for the inside ring, to 1 point, for the outside ring.

Archers use fiberglass bows to shoot steel-tipped graphite or aluminum arrows. Bows have *sights* to help the archers aim, and *stabilizers* to keep the bow steady.

Men and women compete in individual and team events. In the individual competition, the 64 best archers shoot in pairs. The winner advances, and the loser is eliminated. Archers shoot 18 arrows in each of the first three rounds, and 12 arrows in each of the final three rounds.

In the team competition, two countries compete against each other. Three archers per country each shoot nine arrows from 70 meters.

Korea won two gold and two silver medals at the 1992 Olympics, and Korea's Kyung-Chui Lee won the 1995 world championship. Natalia Valeeva, 26, of Moldova is the women's 1995 world champion.

— *by Erin Egan*

Steady doses of heavy-metal music help Jay Barrs of the U.S. steady his bow.

FAST FACTS

- Arrows can zip through the air faster than 150 miles per hour.
- Archery has been called one of the four most important inventions in human history. The others are fire, language, and the wheel.
- An archer scores a "Robin Hood" when he or she shoots an arrow into the shaft of an arrow already in the bull's-eye.

STARS TO WATCH

JAY BARRS, age 34, is rattling archery's image. During competition, most archers try to stay calm and relaxed, which helps them shoot an arrow into a tiny bull's-eye. Jay calls himself a rock-music freak. His specialty is heavy metal. Between rounds, he calms himself by listening to Motley Crüe, Van Halen, and Whitesnake.

The 1996 Olympics will be Jay's third trip to the Games. In 1988, he won the gold medal in the individual competition. In 1992, he finished fifth.

Hitting a bull's-eye is difficult. But it's not as tough as the tricks Jay's friends sometimes ask him to perform. Jay has shot an aspirin off a golf tee, and he has shot an arrow through the hole of one of his old records from 10 yards away.

Badminton

If your idea of badminton is tapping a birdie over a sagging net at a picnic, then you are in for a surprise when you tune in to the Olympics.

In Olympic badminton, players use rackets that look like lightweight tennis rackets to whack a birdie over a net. The net is five feet high. The birdie is also called a shuttlecock. It is made of a one-inch-round piece of cork wrapped in leather and attached to 16 goose feathers.

When the birdie is hit, the feathers squeeze together. The streamlined birdie can hit speeds of 200 miles per hour. Within 20 feet, the feathers open and the birdie can slow to 40 miles per hour.

In the Olympics, men and women compete in singles and doubles, and teams of one man and one woman play mixed doubles. In all events, the goal is to hit the birdie over the net and into the opponent's half of the court so the opponent cannot hit it back. A singles court is 17 feet wide and 44 feet long, and a doubles court is 20 feet wide and 44 feet long.

In all matches except women's singles, games are played to 15 points. Women play to 11 points. A player must win two-out-of-three games to win a match. Players take turns serving, and only the serving player can score. The serve switches when the "hand-in," or serving player or side, fails to score.

Badminton strategy is similar to tennis. Players try to catch opponents out of position by hitting long shots down the line and hard smashes over the net. Good players play patiently, hitting the birdie back over and over until the opponent makes a mistake.

The best players are from Indonesia, Malaysia, China, and Korea. The U.S. is not expected to challenge for medals.

— *by Kara Yorio*

Susi Susanti of Indonesia flicks a gold medal forehand at the 1992 Games.

Fast Facts

- In a doubles match, players can take as many as 50 shots in a 20-second volley.
- Until 1992, Indonesia had never won an Olympic medal. At the 1992 Games, Indonesia badminton players won five medals.
- Badminton became an Olympic sport for the first time in 1992.

Stars to Watch

SUSI SUSANTI is a star in her country of Indonesia. She has a street named after her, and she is a millionaire. No, she's not a rock star or a basketball player. She simply plays badminton better than any other woman in the world.

During the 1992 Olympics, badminton was watched by more people in Indonesia than any other sport. Susi won the gold medal. She also won world championships in 1990, 1991, 1993, 1994, and 1995.

Susi is only 25 years old, and she is favored to win another gold medal in 1996. Her biggest challenge may come from teammate Mia Audina. Mia is only 16 years old. Already, she is being called the next Susi Susanti.

Baseball

Pop quiz: What do major league stars Barry Larkin, Mark McGwire, and Jim Abbott have in common?

Answer: All played baseball in the Olympics before beginning their pro careers.

The Olympics is a great place to watch future big-league stars. Since 1984, 40 Olympic baseball players have gone on to join major league teams. But the 1996 Olympics may be the last time that amateurs will play for the gold medal.

The International Olympic Committee wants pros to play in the next Olympics. There's a good chance the U.S. will send a "Dream Team" of big-league superstars to the 2000 Games in Sydney, Australia.

In Atlanta, eight teams will compete. The teams are the U.S., Cuba, Japan, South Korea, Nicaragua, Italy, Holland, and Australia. Each team will play every other team once in the first round. The four teams with the best records advance to the semifinals. The two winners from the semis will play in the gold medal game.

The playing field and the rules in the Olympics are almost the same as in the major leagues. One difference: Olympic players may use aluminum bats. Designated hitters will bat for pitchers.

Games will be played at Atlanta-Fulton County Stadium, home of the Atlanta Braves. The stadium is called "the launching pad" because it is one of the best big-league parks for hitting home runs. Teams will need good pitching to keep hitters in check.

Pitching is the strength of Team USA, which had a 36–6 record last summer, against some of the teams it will face in Atlanta. The U.S. pitchers are led by right-hander R.A. Dickey, who was 3–1 with a 1.94 earned run average in 1995 for Team USA. Reliever Braden Looper saved six games and had a 1.71 ERA.

The team's offensive star is rightfielder Mark Kotsay. He won the 1995 Golden Spikes Award as the top amateur player in America. He hit .358 with three homers and 31 RBIs last summer.

Catcher A.J. Hinch has played for the U.S. for four years. He has been drafted by

Legend

Want to stump your friends with a baseball trivia question?

Tell them that pitcher Jim Abbott of Team USA beat Japan, 5–3, in the 1988 Olympic gold medal game. Then ask, "Who was Japan's last pitcher in that game?"

The answer is **HIDEO NOMO**, who is now a star for the Los Angeles Dodgers. Hideo pitched the final inning and two thirds of the 1988 gold medal game without allowing a hit or a run.

After the Olympics, Hideo joined the Kintetsu Buffaloes, a Japanese pro team. The Dodgers signed Hideo in 1995 after he retired from the Buffaloes. In 1995, he became the second Japanese player ever to appear in the major leagues. He started in

HIDEO NOMO

the 1995 All-Star Game and won the National League Rookie of the Year Award.

Back in 1988, you would have needed a crystal ball to know that a Japanese pitcher would become a U.S. major league star. That's what makes watching Olympic baseball so much fun.

Fast Facts

- Baseball's rules were written in 1845 by Alexander Cartwright, in New York City. Baseball was introduced in Japan in the 1870's. It is now played in 99 countries.
- Baseball was played as a demonstration sport at the Olympics in 1912, 1936, 1952, 1956, 1964, 1984, and 1988. It became a medal sport in 1992.
- The 1952 U.S. Olympic baseball team was a "pickup" team put together by the coach of the U.S. soccer team. The players were U.S. athletes who were competing in other sports at the Olympics, in Helsinki, Finland. The U.S. beat Finland, 19–1, in its only game.

Stars to Watch

Third baseman **OMAR LINARES** of Cuba belts base hits like Tony Gwynn and has the power of Jose Canseco. He throws with a strong, accurate arm like Ken Griffey, Junior. He's a speedy base runner too.

Major league scouts have called Omar the best amateur baseball player in the world.

Omar, 28, has helped Cuba win four world championships and the 1992 Olympic gold medal. In nine Olympic games, Omar batted .500 and hit four home runs.

Omar was born in Pinar del Rio, Cuba. His father played baseball for a local team, and Omar wanted to follow in his dad's footsteps. At 12, Omar was sent to a special sports school. In 1985, at 17, he became the youngest player ever to make Cuba's national baseball team.

U.S. major league teams would love to have Omar play for them. But he is happy to stay in Cuba. He is his country's most popular player.

International tournaments bring out the best in Omar. He should put on a show in Atlanta.

---

the Chicago White Sox and Minnesota Twins. He turned down both offers to play in the Olympics.

Team USA's toughest opponent will be Cuba, which won the 1992 gold medal. Cuba has dominated international baseball for more than 30 years, but it is showing signs of weakness. At least six of its best players are more than 30 years old. Three of its pitchers have defected to the U.S. so that they can play in the major leagues. Cuba's government rarely allows its people to move to other countries, so they must defect, or escape.

Last summer, Team USA swept Cuba in a four-game series. Cuba had never been swept before.

Is Team USA sure to win the gold medal in Atlanta? Not so fast. Cuba still has plenty of firepower on offense thanks to sluggers Omar Linares *(see Stars to Watch)*, Antonio Pacheco, and Orestes Kindelan. Pitching ace Omar Ajete throws a 95-mile-per-hour fastball.

Japan and Nicaragua are also strong. Japanese players are well-trained in fundamentals such as bunting and defense. Nicaragua has a good offense and solid pitching.

So grab a hot dog, find a seat, and get ready for some excitement.

Play ball!

— *by John Rolfe*

U.S. catcher A.J. Hinch has twice said No to major league teams.

Basketball

It all started in a gym in snowy Springfield, Massachusetts, in 1891. A physical education teacher named Dr. James Naismith was asked to create a game that students could play indoors. Dr. Naismith hung peach baskets at each end of the gym and made a list of rules. Basketball was born.

In 1936, basketball became an Olympic sport. The first Olympic basketball games were played outdoors, on a clay and sand tennis court, in Berlin, Germany. On the day of the final game, between the U.S. and Canada, heavy rain turned the court to mud! The U.S. beat Canada, 19–8.

Until 1992, when professional players from the National Basketball Association (NBA) were allowed to compete in the Olympics, U.S. teams were made up of the country's top college stars. The 1960 team is still thought to be the best amateur team ever. Ten members of that team went on to play in the NBA.

The U.S. men won the first seven Olympic basketball tournaments, from 1936 to 1968. In 1972, the U.S. gold medal streak came to an end. With three seconds left to play in the final game, the U.S. led the Soviet Union, 50–49. The Soviets had the ball. Twice the final seconds ticked down and the U.S. players began to celebrate. But twice the head of the International Amateur Basketball Federation (IABF) decided to reset the clock, giving the Soviets another three seconds to score. On its third try, the Soviet Union scored. The U.S. lost, 51–50.

Basketball was gaining popularity around the world. The players were improving, and several countries had teams that could challenge — or even beat — a squad of U.S. amateur players.

In 1976, the U.S. beat Yugoslavia to regain its Olympic championship. That year, women played basketball in the Olympics for the first time. The Soviet Union won the women's gold medal. The U.S. took the silver and Bulgaria earned the bronze.

Following the U.S. boycott of the 1980 Games, the U.S. won both gold medals in 1984. In 1988, the U.S. women defeated Yugoslavia, 77–70, for the gold medal. Two stars of that team, Teresa Edwards and Katrina McClain, will play for the U.S. in 1996.

Legend

OSCAR ROBERTSON was the first great all-around player to hit the NBA. The 6' 5" guard was a master at shooting, passing, dribbling, rebounding, defense, and teamwork.

Oscar played for the University of Cincinnati from 1957 to 1960. He twice led the Bearcats to the NCAA Final Four. After his final college season, Oscar went to Rome, Italy, to play for the U.S. in the 1960 Olympics. The U.S. won the gold medal easily. The U.S. averaged 102 points per game while opponents averaged only 59.5 points.

After the Games, Oscar joined the Cincinnati Royals of the NBA. Oscar played 10 seasons with the Royals and four years with the Milwaukee Bucks. In Milwaukee, Oscar teamed up with Kareem Abdul-Jabbar. They led the Bucks to the 1970–71 NBA championship.

Oscar averaged 26 points per game during his 14-year pro career. He was the league MVP once and an All-Star 12 times.

OSCAR ROBERTSON

The U.S. men were not so fortunate. Ever since it lost to the Soviet Union in the final game of the 1972 Olympic tournament, the U.S had been waiting for a chance to settle the score. In 1988, the U.S. and the Soviet Union met in the semi-finals. The U.S. team included future NBA stars David Robinson, Mitch Richmond, Danny Manning, Charles Smith, and Dan Majerle. But it wasn't enough. The Soviets, led by Sarunas Marciulionis, now with the Sacramento Kings, built up a 10-point lead by halftime and coasted to an 82–76 victory.

The U.S. had learned its lesson. The 1988 team was the last men's amateur Olympic team to play for the U.S. in the Olympics. In 1992, the U.S. sent a Dream Team of NBA players to the Olympics to make sure the U.S. won the gold medal.

After losing to the Unified Team in the semi-finals of the 1992 Olympics, the U.S. women assembled a Dream

Shaquille O'Neal is a huge reason why the U.S. should romp.

Team of their own. That team will play in 1996.

U.S. players must make some adjustments to play in the Olympics.

♦ In the Olympics, the 3-point line is 20 feet 6 inches from the basket. The NBA line is 22 feet from the basket, while the college line is 19 feet 9 inches away.

♦ The Olympic shot clock buzzes at 30 seconds. Colleges also use the 30-second clock, but NBA players are used to a 24-second clock.

♦ Olympic players foul out with their fifth foul, which is the same for college players but one fewer than are allowed in the NBA.

♦ The foul lane in the Olympics is wider near the basket than it is near the foul line. Centers must post up farther from the basket, which helps to open the lane for drives to the hoop.

NBA players will also face zone defenses, and the court is slightly smaller than an NBA or a college floor. Games in the Olympics are broken into 20-minute halves, which is the same as U.S. college games. NBA players are used to playing four 12-minute quarters.

FAST FACTS

● Who holds the Olympic record for most points in a game? Oscar Schmidt of Brazil scored 55 points in a 1988 game against Spain. He averaged 42 points per game for the tournament.

● In 1976, Uljana Semjonova of the Soviet Union averaged 19.4 points and 12.4 rebounds per game. She was 6' 10½" tall and weighed 260 pounds.

● The U.S. men won 62 Olympic games in a row from 1936 to 1972.

Men

The Dream is back. In 1992, when professional players were first allowed to play in the Olympics, the U.S. Dream Team romped to the gold medal. Among the team's stars were Michael Jordan, Larry Bird, and Magic Johnson. The U.S. won each of its games, in Barcelona, Spain, by an average of 44 points. The real competition was the battle for second place, which was won by Croatia.

In 1996, the latest edition of the Dream Team should streak through the Olympic tournament just as easily. Returning from the 1992 Dream Team are Karl Malone, John Stockton, Scottie Pippen, and David Robinson. Joining them are Shaquille O'Neal, Penny Hardaway, Reggie Miller, Glenn Robinson, Hakeem Olajuwon, and Grant Hill. The final two spots on the roster will be filled in the spring before the Olympics begin.

Of course, the U.S. is not the only team in the Olympic tournament. The other 11 teams are Australia, Argentina, Croatia, Lithuania, Angola, Puerto Rico, Brazil, China, South Korea, Yugoslavia, and Greece.

In addition to Dream Team members, several other NBA players will compete for their home countries *against* the United States. Toni Kukoc *(see Stars to Watch, page 13)* of the Chicago Bulls and Dino Radja of the Boston Celtics will play for Croatia. Vlade Divac of the

FAST FACTS

● David Robinson is the first male U.S. basketball player to play in three Olympics.
● Lithuania did not have enough money to buy uniforms for its 1992 Olympic team. The music group the Grateful Dead donated tie-dyed uniforms. Lithuania won the bronze medal.
● Reggie Miller's sister, Cheryl, won an Olympic gold medal with the U.S. women's basketball team in 1984.

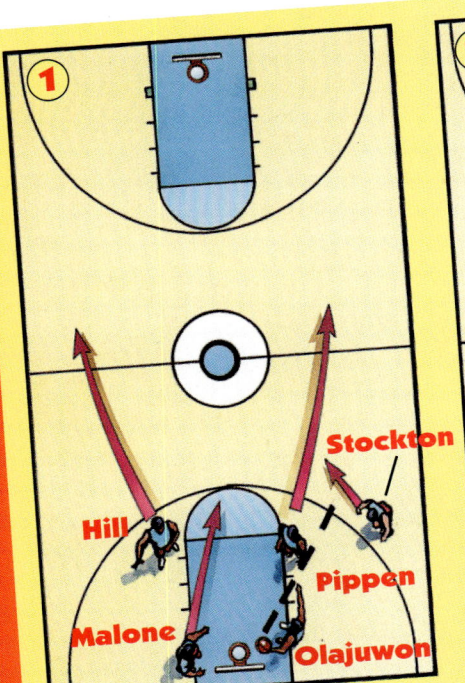

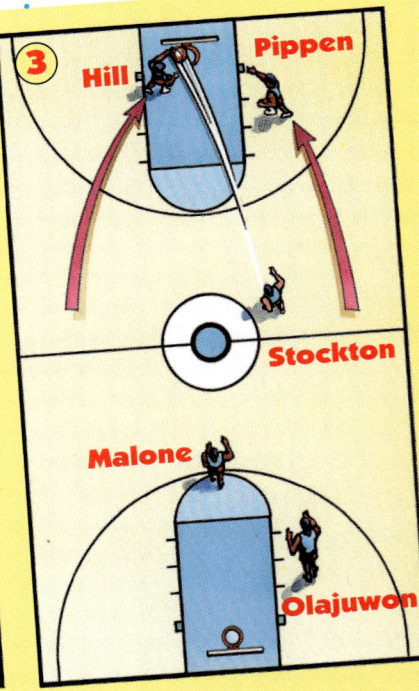

DREAM TEAM FAST BREAK

The Dream Team has so much talent and speed that a simple fast break will be a major nightmare for opponents. Here's how a Dream Team fast break might work. **1.** Hakeem Olajuwon grabs a rebound and throws an outlet pass to guard John Stockton. Forwards Grant Hill and Scottie Pippen sprint down the floor on opposite sides of the court. **2.** John dribbles quickly down the center of the court. Grant and Scottie run ahead of John. **3.** John can either drive to the basket, stop and shoot, or fake a shot to pull the defense toward him and pass to Grant or Scottie for an easy jam.

Los Angeles Lakers will play for Yugoslavia. Sarunas Marciulionis of the Sacramento Kings will play for Lithuania. And Luc Longley of the Chicago Bulls will play for Australia.

After the U.S., the strongest teams are from Lithuania, Croatia, and Yugoslavia. All three appear to be equally matched.

The world will certainly be watching games between Croatia and Yugoslavia. Until 1991, Croatia was part of Yugoslavia. Croatian players such as Toni Kukoc used to be teammates and friends with Yugoslavian players such as Vlade Divac.

But in 1991, Croatia broke away from Yugoslavia to form its own country. Yugoslavia attacked Croatia to keep it from leaving. Because it started a war, Yugoslavia was not allowed to compete in the Olympics in 1992.

The U.S. has so much talent that it can play any style of game it wants. The team can throw the ball to Hakeem, Shaq, or David Robinson in the low post and let them work one-on-one. John Stockton and Karl Malone can run the pick-and-roll. Reggie Miller can break around screens and shoot 3-pointers. And Scottie Pippen and Penny Hardaway can lead the sonic-speed fast break.

Opposing teams simply do not have the talent to match the United States. European teams hope to overcome the overall talent of the U.S. team with set plays run with precision, accurate long-range shooting, and clogging zone defenses. Many players on opposing teams have also played together for years, and they are familiar with international rules. Still, the question is not: Will the U.S. win the gold medal? But rather: By how much?

In the Olympics, Chicago Bull Toni Kukoc plays for Croatia.

Stars to Watch

In the 1992 Olympics, **TONI KUKOC** [KOO-coach] played for his home country of Croatia. When Croatia played the U.S., Michael Jordan and Scottie Pippen of the Chicago Bulls tried to make Toni look bad. They were upset because Toni had been offered a contract by the Bulls. They didn't think Toni was ready for the NBA.

In Croatia's first game against the U.S., Toni played badly and the U.S. won, 103–70. A week later, the U.S. and Croatia met again, this time in the gold medal game.

Before that game, Larry Bird told Toni, "If you have it, now's the time to show it." Toni had it. He scored 16 points in Croatia's 117–85 loss to the United States.

Toni, a 6' 11" forward, joined the Bulls following the 1993 season. Now Scottie and Michael are happy he is their teammate.

Women

In 1992, the U.S. women's basketball team started training together just before the Olympics. The U.S. team was made up of the best players in the country. U.S. teams had won gold medals in 1984 and 1988, and anything less than the gold in 1992 would be a surprise.

But in the semi-finals of the Olympic tournament, the U.S. lost to the Unified Team, 79–73. The U.S. ended up with the bronze medal, and the Unified Team beat China for the gold.

U.S. players and officials were extremely disappointed that the team did not win the gold. But the team learned a valuable lesson.

"The rest of the world has not only caught up to the United States in women's basketball," says U.S. coach Tara VanDerveer. "They have passed us."

The U.S. does not plan to be disappointed in 1996. The team that the U.S. is sending to Atlanta should be the strongest U.S. women's team ever to play together on one court.

The team was selected in 1995. The best players in the country were invited to Colorado Springs, Colorado, to try out for the U.S. Women's National Team. After a week of workouts, 11 players were named to the team. Most of the players are former college stars. Nine have played for professional teams in Europe and Japan. Some have earned as much as $200,000 a year. To play for the U.S. team, each would be paid $50,000.

In the summer of 1995 — a full year before the Olympics — the players began training together. Then came games against U.S. college teams and national teams from Olympic competitors such as China and Russia.

The team's goal was clear: to win the Olympic gold medal in Atlanta.

The U.S. is led by Teresa Edwards, a 31-year-old guard who has already played in three Olympics. Center Katrina McClain played in the 1988 and 1992 Games. She was the leading rebounder for the U.S. in the 1992 Olympics. Teresa and Katrina were teammates at the University of Georgia.

The big gun for the U.S. could be 6' 5" forward Lisa Leslie. In high school, she

Fast Facts

- Zaire is the first team from Africa to qualify for the Olympic women's basketball tournament.
- Teresa Edwards is the only basketball player ever to play in four Olympics.
- At the Olympics, basketball players may wear only numbers 4 through 15.
- Women's basketball is very popular in Europe. Professional players can earn more than $250,000 a year.
- In the Olympics, only the coach can call time out.

Legend

LYNETTE WOODARD

In 1984, **LYNETTE WOODARD** helped the U.S. win its first ever Olympic gold medal in women's basketball. But Lynette is better known for what she did *after* the Games. In 1985, she became the first woman to play for the Harlem Globetrotters.

The Globetrotters were formed in 1926. They travel around the world playing basketball games that are full of tricks and fun. Players must be nifty ball handlers, great passers, and tremendous shooters. Lynette beat out 17 top women players for the position on the team.

"It was unbelievable," says Lynette. She traveled around the world to perform, and she met people such as the Pope, Michael Jackson, and Whitney Houston. "These are people I idolized," says Lynette.

Lynette played for the Globetrotters for two years. But she says playing in the Olympics is still her greatest basketball memory.

"To hear the crowds going berserk, chanting 'U-S-A, U-S-A!' . . . that was fantastic!" Lynette says.

once scored 101 points — in the first half. During the 1994–95 season, she averaged 22 points and 11.7 rebounds a game for a professional team in Italy.

Other members of the team include Sheryl Swoopes *(see Stars to Watch),* who led Texas Tech to the national college championship in 1993, and Rebecca Lobo, who led the University of Connecticut to the college championship two years later.

The Olympic tournament features 12 teams: the U.S., Australia, Brazil, Canada, China, Cuba, Italy, Japan, Russia, South Korea, Ukraine, and Zaire.

Russia should offer the strongest challenge to the United States. Several Russian players competed for the Unified Team in 1992, including point guard Irina Sumnikova. Irina Rutkovskaya was Russia's leading scorer at the 1994 Goodwill Games.

China is also a medal contender. China boasts one of the world's most powerful centers in 6' 9" Haixia Zheng. Haixia is not agile or quick, but she is a force under the basket because of her size. She was the Most Outstanding Player of the 1994 world championships.

Ukraine, like Russia, has several players from the 1992 Unified Team. With its experience, excellent 3-point shooting, and rebounding, Ukraine could battle for a medal.

Women's basketball joined the Olympics in 1976. The 1996 Olympic tournament could be the best yet.

— *by Kara Yorio*

Guard Sheryl Swoopes leads the U.S. charge for the gold medal.

Stars to Watch

Put away your Air Jordans, there's a new shoe on the shelves. Air Swoopes — the first basketball shoe named after a woman — hit the stores in October 1995. The shoe is named after U.S. guard **SHERYL SWOOPES** (her last name rhymes with hoops).

Sheryl, 25, grew up in Brownfield, Texas. When she was 7, she began playing basketball against her two older brothers, James and Earl. In 1993, she led Texas Tech to the national college championship. Sheryl scored a championship-game record of 47 points in the final, leading Texas Tech to an 84–82 win over Ohio State. "Air Swoopes" was voted MVP of the tournament and National Player of the Year. She averaged 28 points per game for the season.

Sheryl would like to be a sports broadcaster when her basketball career is over. But first comes a stop in Atlanta. "All I'm thinking of is the 1996 gold medal," says Sheryl.

Boxing

Ladies and gentlemen! In this corner is one of the world's oldest sports . . . boxing! It was part of the Ancient Olympics, in Greece, more than 2,000 years ago. In 1904, boxing became a modern Olympic sport. This year, 364 fighters will put on a show of strength, speed, and strategy.

Olympic boxing is a little different from pro boxing. For starters, it's less dangerous. Olympic boxers wear gear to protect their heads. If a boxer is clearly out-matched and in danger of being clobbered, the referee will stop the bout.

An Olympic fighter must be between the ages of 17 and 32. He can compete in one of 12 weight classes. The lightest is light-flyweight (106 pounds). The heaviest is super-heavyweight (more than 201 pounds).

Olympic matches last up to three rounds. (Most pro fights are 12 rounds.) Each round is three minutes long. If a fighter wins a match, he advances to the next match. To win the gold medal, a fighter must win five matches. If he loses once, he's out of the competition.

The matches are controlled by a referee. Part of the ref's job is to make sure fighters obey the rules. They may not hit below the belt, on the back, or when an opponent is down or too dazed to defend himself.

Knockouts are rare in the Olympics. Most fighters win by outscoring opponents. Judges award points based on the number of fair, clean punches a fighter lands. The *number* of punches is more important than the power of the punches. Only punches that land on the body or the front of the head count. Each glove has a large, white patch on the front of the fist. A fighter must hit his opponent with this part of the glove for the punch to count.

If the score is tied at the end of a bout, judges can award the round to the most aggressive fighter. Good defense is also important. A fighter can win a close round by blocking punches with his gloves, ducking, and dancing out of danger.

Olympic competition is open only to amateurs. All-time greats such as Muhammad Ali *(see Legend)*, Sugar Ray Leonard, and George Foreman, as well as current pros Evander Holyfield and Oscar de la Hoya, fought in the Olympics before turning pro. The boxing tournament in

Legend

In 1960, an 18-year old boxer named Cassius Clay went to the Olympics with a dream of winning a gold medal. His dream came true when he beat everyone in the light-heavyweight division. He later became the best-known athlete in the world.

After turning pro, Cassius fought heavyweight champion Sonny Liston, in 1964. Cassius beat the champ. After the bout, he declared himself "The Greatest." Cassius also was deeply interested in the Muslim religion, and he changed his name to **MUHAMMAD ALI.**

Muhammad was drafted into the U.S. military in 1966. He refused to go, on the grounds that he was a Muslim minister. He was sent to jail and boxing officials took his title away. In 1970, Muhammad was found innocent and was allowed to box again.

MUHAMMAD ALI

In 1974, Muhammad beat George Foreman for the heavyweight championship. He lost the title, won it back, lost again, and won for a third time in 1978. Muhammad Ali was the first boxer ever to win the world heavyweight title three times. To many boxing fans, he really was "The Greatest."

Cuba's Felix Savon *(in blue)* is the world's best amateur fighter.

Atlanta should be an exciting showdown between the U.S. and Cuba. The U.S. has won more Olympic boxing medals (96) than any other country. Cuba has been a force since 1972. It has won 34 Olympic medals even though it did not compete at the 1984 or 1988 Games.

The U.S. boxing team is led by Antonio Tarver, the world's top-ranked light-heavyweight (178 pounds). Last year, Antonio became the first American boxer ever to win U.S., world, and Pan Am Games championships in the same year.

Two of America's most promising boxers are flyweight (112 pounds) Eric Morel and light-welterweight (139 pounds) Fernando Vargas. Fernando is only 18, but he is already ranked Number 1 in the U.S. in his weight class.

Cuba dominated the 1995 world championships by winning four gold, two silver, and three bronze medals. Five Cuban boxers were ranked Number 1 in the world last year. Expect big things from Cuba's Felix Savon *(see Stars to Watch)*.

The U.S. and Cuba won't be the only strong teams in Atlanta. Fighters from Germany, Russia, and Bulgaria all have a fighting chance to win Olympic boxing medals.

— *by John Rolfe*

Fast Facts

- **Boxers are sometimes called pugs.** "The nickname comes from the word "pugilist" [PYOO-juh-list]. It's Latin for "a person who fights with his hands."
- **When a fighter is knocked down or is dazed, the referee counts out loud.** If the fighter doesn't recover before the ref says eight, the fight is over.
- **Eddie Eagan, the 1920 light-heavyweight gold medalist, is the only athlete to win gold medals at Summer and Winter Olympics.** Eagan also won a gold medal as a bobsledder, in 1932.

Stars to Watch

As an 8-year-old, **FELIX SAVON** watched on TV as Cuban heavyweight Teofilo Stevenson won the 1976 Olympic gold medal. Ten years later, Felix and Teofilo were teammates on Cuba's national team.

"He was my idol," Felix once said. "I could never imagine that I would be his teammate."

Felix is now the best amateur boxer in the world. His powerful punches and quick reflexes have helped him win five heavyweight world championships. He will defend his 1992 Olympic gold medal in Atlanta.

Felix grew up in San Vicente, Cuba. At 13, he went to a sports school and learned to box. He has won more than 276 matches in his career.

Canoe/Kayak

One word describes the difference between paddling a canoe around a lake and the canoe and kayak races you will see in the Olympics. That word is *supercharged*.

In the Olympics, the boats are supercharged, the races are supercharged, and the awesome Olympic paddlers are supercharged.

Canoes and kayaks race on two types of water, flatwater and whitewater. Flatwater races are held on a calm, smooth lake. A course has nine lanes, and races are 500 meters and 1,000 meters long. The Olympic flatwater races will be held on Lake Lanier, which is about 50 miles from Atlanta. Flatwater events are also called sprints.

Whitewater races are held on a river with fast-moving water, called rapids or whitewater. The Olympic races will be held on the Ocoee River, in Ocoee, Tennessee, which is about 130 miles north of Atlanta. Whitewater events are also called slalom.

Canoe competition in flatwater and whitewater is held for one-man and two-man boats. A flatwater doubles canoe is 20 feet long and 30 inches wide, and weighs 44 pounds. A singles canoe is slightly smaller. Canoes have an open deck, and paddlers kneel on the bottom on one knee. Canoe paddles have a blade on one end, and a paddler propels his canoe by stroking on one side of the canoe.

A kayak is the same length as a canoe, but it is a few pounds lighter and only 20 inches wide. This helps make it slightly faster. Men and women race singles, doubles, and four-person kayaks in flatwater, and singles in whitewater.

A kayak has a covered deck, and the paddler sits on the bottom of the kayak. A kayaker uses a paddle with a blade at each

GATE CRASHERS
The Olympic whitewater races are exciting, wild, and wet. The 415-meter-long course will be set on the Ocoee River, in Tennessee. *(A section of the course is shown above.)* Paddlers steer around rocks, through fast-moving water, and between the 25 gates marking the course. Each gate is two poles suspended above the water, five feet apart. A paddler's head and shoulders must pass between the poles. A few of the gates are upriver gates. These are tricky. Paddlers must turn around and paddle *against* the current to go through them.

Scott Shipley of the U.S. steers his kayak through the gates.

end. The kayaker holds the middle of the paddle and propels the kayak by stroking on one side and then the other.

The Olympic course is 415 meters long and has 25 gates. Each gate consists of two poles, which the paddlers must paddle between. The poles are about five feet apart and hang six inches above the river.

Whitewater paddlers need tremendous strength and skill. The river is full of large rocks and tricky, swirling water. Paddlers go down the river one boat at a time, and the fastest time wins. If a paddler hits a gate, five seconds are added to his time. If the paddler misses a gate, or goes through the gates in the wrong order or the wrong direction, 50 seconds are added to his time.

In flatwater kayaking, Knut Holmann of Norway is a favorite in the 500-meter and 1,000-meter singles events. He won a bronze medal and a silver medal in 1992.

Defending champion Nikolai Buhalov of Bulgaria is favored in singles canoe.

Birgit Schmidt of Germany and Rita Koban of Hungary are expected to battle for the gold medal in women's flatwater kayak. Birgit won the gold medal at the 1992 Olympics. Rita won the gold medal at the 1995 world championships.

Scott Shipley of the U.S. *(see Stars to Watch)* is among the favorites in whitewater kayak. Lukas Pollert of the Czech Republic is the defending gold medalist in whitewater canoe. Jon Lugbill of the U.S. dominated whitewater canoe racing from 1979 to 1992. At the 1992 Olympics, he touched a gate and finished fourth. He is making a comeback after a brief retirement.

Dana Chladek of the U.S. won a bronze medal in women's kayak in 1992 and hopes to turn that into gold in 1996.

— *by Kara Yorio*

STARS TO WATCH

When **SCOTT SHIPLEY** was 12, his parents went to Los Angeles, California, to watch the 1984 Olympics. Scott went to his bedroom. He drew the Olympic rings, and then wrote "Paris 1992". His goal was to make the Olympic team eight years later.

Scott started paddling at age six and began competing when he was 11. He practiced as often as he could. In 1992, he made the U.S. Olympic team. He finished 27th in whitewater kayak at the Games in Barcelona, Spain.

Scott has improved a lot since 1992. In 1995, he finished second at the world championships. That race was held on the Ocoee River, site of the Olympics.

Cycling

The goal in all Olympic cycling events is, of course, to win. To do that, cyclists need to know when to pedal hard and when to *coast*.

In the Olympics, men and women race on the streets of Atlanta and on a track called a velodrome. The velodrome is a wooden oval with banked curves, 250 meters around.

♦ **Road race:** The riders (200 in the men's event, 60 in the women's race) start together. Men race 17 laps around the 8.1-mile course, and women race eight laps.

In the road race, cyclists spend most of the race riding in a pack. Air resistance makes it harder for a cyclist to ride alone. By riding behind another cyclist, a rider can save 30 percent of his energy. This is called drafting.

Throughout the race, cyclists will *try* to get away from the main pack. Most of these breakaways will be caught. But the course in Atlanta has a lot of corners. If a group of riders gets around a corner and out of sight, the pack may not catch them. If the pack stays together, the finish will be a furious sprint at speeds of 40 miles per hour.

In the men's race, Lance Armstrong of the U.S. is one of several riders strong enough to win. Jeannie Longo of France is the women's world champion.

♦ **Time trial:** Racers start one-at-a-time, every two minutes. Riders are not allowed to draft, and the rider with the fastest time wins. Men ride four loops of the road course, or 32.4 miles; women ride two laps, or 16.2 miles.

Miguel Induráin of Spain *(see Stars to Watch, page 21)* is the strongest time-trial rider in the world. Jeannie Longo of France should win the women's event.

♦ **1,000-meter time trial:** This men-only track event is similar to the time trial. Riders start one-at-a-time and ride four laps. The fastest time wins. Erin Hartwell of the U.S. won the bronze medal at the 1992 Olympics.

♦ **4,000-meter team pursuit:** Two teams of four riders (men only) each start on opposite sides of the track. A team wins by finishing first, or by catching and passing the other team. The winning team advances to the next round. The world's top teams are from Australia, the United States, and Ukraine.

♦ **Sprint:** Men and women race two-at-a-time for three laps, or 750 meters. For most of the race, riders pedal slowly, watching the other rider.

WIND BREAKERS
In some events, cyclists ride alone. Their greatest challenge is cutting through the wind. **1.** In those events, a cyclist rides a bike with aerodynamic features, such as a solid rear wheel, smaller front wheel, bladed frame tubes, and handlebars that put a rider into a sleek position, similar to a ski-racer's tuck. **2.** Cyclists in the road race ride normal racing bikes.

Fast Facts

- In Atlanta, professionals will compete in Olympic cycling events for the first time.
- Men have competed in cycling in every modern Olympics except 1904. Women first competed in an Olympic road race in 1984 and a track race in 1988.
- The men's road race at the 1912 Olympics was 320 kilometers, or 199 miles, long. The race started at 2 A.M. and was won by Rudolph "Okey" Lewis of South Africa. His time: 10 hours 42 minutes 39 seconds.

Miguel Induráin of Spain has won the Tour de France five times.

With about 200 meters left, they sprint. The first rider across the finish line wins. Felicia Ballanger of France is the women's world champion. Among the men, Marty Nothstein of the U.S. should battle world champion Darryn Hill of Australia for the gold medal.

◆ **Individual pursuit:** This event is identical to the team pursuit, except riders race alone. Men race 4,000 meters, or 16 laps around the track, and women race 3,000 meters, or 12 laps. Two cyclists start at opposite sides of the track. To win, a rider must either finish first or catch and pass the other rider. Rebecca Twigg of the U.S. won the 1995 women's world championship, and Graeme Obree of Great Britain won the men's event.

◆ **Points race:** Women ride 100 laps around the track and men race 160 laps. Every eighth lap is a sprint lap. Points are awarded to the riders who finish the lap first, second, third, and fourth. Double points are awarded on the final lap. The rider with the most points wins. Italy's Silvio Martinelli is favored in the men's race. World champion Svetlana Samokhvalova is favored in the women's event.

— *by Kara Yorio*

Stars to Watch

★ Professional cyclists will compete in the Olympics for the first time in 1996. That gives Olympic fans a chance to see one of the greatest cyclists ever — **MIGUEL INDURAIN** of Spain.

Miguel, age 32, has won the Tour de France each of the past five years. This is cycling's most important race. Riders race 21 to 24 days and cover more than 2,000 miles. Miguel is the only rider ever to win the race five times in a row.

Miguel is a powerful rider, and he can win on almost any course. But he is strongest in the time-trial event, in which cyclists ride alone and the fastest time wins. Miguel is the world champion in this event.

Miguel grew up in Spain, where cycling is very popular. He is one of his country's greatest sports heroes. At 6' 2" tall and 175 pounds, Miguel is bigger than most cyclists. Riders call him "Extraterrestrial" because his riding ability is "out of this world."

Mountain Biking

Mountain-bike racing is a sport a bunch of kids might invent. You jump on a bike with fat, mud-grabbing tires and race up and down hills. You fly off jumps and hop over logs. The first rider across the finish line wins.

In 1996, mountain biking becomes an Olympic sport for the first time. Men and women will compete in cross-country events. Men will race six to seven laps of the 5.5-mile course, and women will race five to six laps.

Most mountain-bike courses have huge climbs that spread out the riders. The Atlanta course is different. It features some hills and a lot of obstacles. It is designed to test bike-handling skills and endurance, but the course will not spread the field. This means the finish could end in a sprint, which is unusual in mountain biking.

Juli Furtado of the U.S. pedals for gold in mountain biking.

Fifty riders will compete in the men's race, and 30 will race in the women's event.

Mountain bikes are made for the rough stuff. They have strong, lightweight frames, 24 gears, and front suspension to keep riders steady on bumps. Riders must carry spare tubes and repair their own flat tires.

Race strategy varies from rider to rider. Many sprint at the start to break away from the pack. They know it is difficult to pass on the narrow trails later in the race. Other riders start slowly and hope to catch those who start fast but tire and slow down.

Among the men, David "Tinker" Juarez is a two-time U.S. champion. Thomas Frischknecht of Switzerland has won two World Cup championships, and Henrik Djernis of Denmark has twice won the world championship.

In the women's event, two riders lead the pack. Juli Furtado *(see Stars to Watch)* is a three-time U.S. champion, and Alison Sydor of Canada has won the world championship the past two years.

— *by Kara Yorio*

★ Stars to Watch ★

Mountain biking may be new to the Olympics, but it is not new for 29-year-old **JULI FURTADO** of the United States. She has been racing on the mud and rocks for six years.

As a teenager, Juli was a downhill ski racer. Her goal was to compete in the Winter Olympics. But after a series of knee injuries, she began riding a bike to strengthen her knee. In 1989, she won cycling's national championship in road racing.

In 1990, Juli switched to mountain biking. The former downhill skier quickly became one of the best at pedaling *up* steep mountains. Juli has won a world championship and three national championships. Her goal now: an Olympic gold medal.

Equestrian

Heat will be a factor for all the athletes in Atlanta. But athletes in the equestrian events — the horses — could have the most trouble of all.

Horses overheat easily. To keep horses safe, events will be held in the mornings, stalls will have fans, and horses and riders will be sprayed with water during events.

In equestrian events, Olympic or otherwise, men and women compete together. Athletes compete in three events: dressage [dress-AHGE], show jumping, and three-day. Individual and team events are held in each event. In team events, four horses and riders from each country compete.

Dressage tests how well a horse responds to a rider while performing a difficult series of moves. Riders wear formal jackets and top hats.

In **show jumping**, a horse is guided around a course that has 15 to 20 obstacles for the horse to jump. The obstacles include walls, poles, gates, and a water jump. Speed is important, but a horse and rider lose points each time the horse touches or knocks down an obstacle.

The **three-day event** is a test of three skills: dressage, endurance, and jumping. Each section takes place on a separate day.

Nicole Uphoff-Becker of

Germany's Ludger Beerbaum and his horse fly over tall obstacles.

Germany won individual and team gold medals in dressage in 1988 and 1992.

Franke Sloothaak (*see Stars to Watch*) and his German teammate Ludger Beerbaum are among the top show jumpers in the world.

U.S. rider Bruce Davidson has won two gold medals and one silver medal in five Olympics in the three-day team event.

Three-day event rider Mark Todd of New Zealand won the individual gold medal at the 1984 and 1988 Olympics.

— *by Erin Egan*

Stars to Watch

⭐ Show-jumper **FRANKE SLOOTHAAK** [FRAHN-keh SLOO-tahk] of Germany and his horse Weihaiwej [WAY-uh-way] are quite a team.

Franke is the Number 1 show jumper in the world. He began riding Weihaiwej in 1993. The next year, they won the individual show-jumping event at the world championships. They also helped Germany win the team event.

Franke, age 38, was born in the Netherlands, but he became a German citizen in 1979. He won a bronze medal at the 1984 Olympics and gold in 1988, in the team competition.

Weihaiwej has a white face and an unusual characteristic for a horse — blue eyes.

Fencing

Next to gymnastics, fencing may be the most graceful Olympic sport. Fencers must be quick, agile, and smart.

Men fencers compete in three individual events, each requiring a different sword: foil, épée, and sabre. Women compete in foil and épée. Fencers also compete in five-person team events.

The goal in fencing is to touch your opponent with your weapon.

◆ **Foil:** The foil weighs less than a pound, is about 43 inches long, and is flexible. A foil fencer must hit an opponent on the torso with the tip of the sword. Hits to the head, arms, or legs do not count. Only the fencer who starts an attack may score. A defense against an attack is a "parry."

◆ **Epée:** The épée *[eh-PAY]* is heavier than the foil and has a stiff blade. Points are scored by touching an opponent on the body with the tip. If both fencers touch at the same time, both score points.

Grigori Kirienko of Russia *(left)* will take a stab at winning the gold medal in sabre.

FAST FACTS

● From 1932 to 1960, Aladar Gerevich of Hungary won six team gold medals and one individual gold medal in the sabre.

● Before electronic scoring was introduced in the 1930's, touches were determined by an ink spot left on the fencer's uniform by the sword. That's why fencers started wearing white uniforms.

◆ **Sabre:** The sabre is light and stiff. Touches are scored by a hit with the tip or the edge above the waist, including the head. (Don't worry: The blade is not sharp and fencers wear protective clothes.)

The first fencer to score five touches within six minutes wins. If neither scores five touches, the fencer with the most touches wins.

Among the men, Dmitri Chevtchenko of Russia and Elvis Gregory Gil of Cuba are favored in foil. Eric Srecki of France *(see Stars to Watch)* is the favorite in épée. Grigori Kirienko of Russia is the world's best sabre fencer.

Among women, Giovanna Trillini of Italy and Laura Badea of Romania are the top foil fencers. Gyongyi Szalay of Hungary and Leslie Marx of the U.S. will compete with several women in épée.

— *by Bob Der*

STARS TO WATCH

★ **ERIC SRECKI** of France is one of the most consistent épée fencers in the world. He won gold medals at the 1992 Olympics and at the 1995 world championships.

Eric, age 31, started fencing when he was 6. His father was in the French army, so Eric was able to take lessons at a military academy in Paris, France.

Eric studied law for five years at the Sorbonne *[sawr-BAHN]*, a famous college in Paris. After graduation, he went to work at the National Bank of Paris.

Eric works at the bank in the morning, practices with the French fencing team in the afternoon, and trains with a personal coach at night.

Eric enjoys movies and music. He likes the Rolling Stones, Mel Gibson, and Harrison Ford.

Field Hockey

In the U.S., field hockey is a relatively unknown sport. It is played by girls and women in high schools and colleges, but very few men play. This is not true in much of the rest of the world. In countries such as India and Pakistan, field hockey is as popular as baseball is in the United States.

Field hockey has often been called soccer with a stick. Two teams of 10 players and a goalie play on a field about the size of a football field. At each end of the field are soccer-sized goals. Players use sticks with a curve at one end to dribble, pass, and shoot a three-inch, hard-plastic ball.

Teams score in three ways:

◆ Field shots are taken from inside the striking circle. This is a semicircle 16 yards from the goal for men and 10 yards for women.

◆ A penalty corner is awarded when a player is accidentally fouled inside the striking circle, or intentionally fouled between the striking circle and the 25-yard line. A player standing at the goal line hits the ball to a teammate kneeling outside the striking circle. The kneeling player stops the ball, and a third player tries to hit it past the goalie.

◆ A penalty stroke is awarded when an offensive player is fouled intentionally inside the striking circle, or when an unintentional foul prevents a goal. One player shoots from seven yards in front of the goal.

In Atlanta, 12 men's teams and eight women's teams will compete.

– by Erin Egan

U.S. captain Barb Marois will retire after the Olympics. Will she retire with a medal?

Fast Facts

● Players hit the ball at speeds of up to 100 miles per hour. Players wear shin guards and goalies wear pads and a mask.
● Men's hockey first appeared in the Olympics in 1908. Women's hockey joined in 1980.
● The U.S. men's and women's teams failed to qualify for the 1992 Olympics.
● In 17 Olympics, India has won eight gold, one silver, and two bronze medals. The gold medals are the only gold medals India has won in the Olympics.

Stars to Watch

The U.S. women's team was ranked third in the world in 1995. That was the team's highest ranking since 1984, when it won an Olympic bronze medal.

BARB MAROIS [ma-ROYCE], age 33, is the captain of the U.S team. She plays sweeper, and her job is to organize the defense. Barb has played for the national team since 1986. She does hundreds of push-ups and sit-ups every day to stay in shape. She also runs about 25 miles a week.

Argentina, Australia, and Korea should battle the U.S. women for medals.

The U.S. men's team is not a threat to win a medal. Australia is favored. Pakistan, India, and Germany are also strong.

Gymnastics

Just how popular is Olympic gymnastics? It's so popular that fans in Atlanta are paying $22 for tickets to watch the gymnasts *practice*.

Gymnastics has been a men's Olympic event since 1896 and a women's event since 1928. Early men's events included the rope-climb and club-swinging. It wasn't until the 1924 Games that medals were awarded in individual events as well as team and all-around.

The team event was the only women's event until 1952.

Gymnastics has always been a popular Olympic sport. But its popularity began to soar in 1972. That's when Olga Korbut of the Soviet Union *(see Legend, page 28)* flipped across TV screens around the world. In 1976, Nadia Comaneci of Romania scored the first perfect 10 in Olympic history. At the 1984 Games, Mary Lou Retton became the first U.S. gymnast to win a gold medal in the all-around event.

In team competition, six of a country's seven gymnasts compete in each event, and the top five scores count. Each athlete performs a compulsory and an optional routine in each event. Compulsory routines are the same for every athlete. Each gymnast creates his or her optional routine. The team with the most points wins.

The 36 top-scoring gymnasts from the team event advance to the all-around. In the all-around, each gymnast performs one optional routine in each event. The gymnast's scores from each event are added together to get the all-around score.

The top eight in each event in the team competition advance to the individual event finals. Gymnasts perform their optional routines. Six judges score each event.

Legend

While performing his floor-exercise routine during the team competition at the 1976 Olympics, **SHUN FUJIMOTO** injured his right leg. He had just done a flip, and his leg twisted when he landed. He knew the leg was broken.

Shun also knew that he wanted Japan to beat the Soviet Union in the team event. So he did not tell anyone about his injury.

Shun's next event was the pommel horse. He scored 9.5. Next up was the rings event. Shun's routine was excellent. For his dismount, Shun swung 10 feet into the air. He flipped and twisted, then landed on his feet.

The pain shot up his leg. He could not hide his agony as he hobbled off the mat. Shun earned an amazing 9.7 in the event.

Shun could not continue, but his scores helped Japan win the gold medal.

SHUN FUJIMOTO

Shun became a hero because of his dedication, but his injury forced him give up gymnastics.

Years later, a reporter asked Shun if he would do the same thing again if he knew how much it would hurt. His anwer? "No!"

Fast Facts

- The vaulting horse got its name because in the early days of gymnastics, soldiers would vault over real horses!
- In 1922, track-and-field events were part of the world gymnastics championships. Events like the pole vault, shot put, and 100-meter sprint were included. The last track events were dropped from the world gymnastics championships in 1954.

Men

In addition to team and all-around, men compete in six individual events: floor exercise, pommel horse, still rings, vault, parallel bars, and horizontal bar.

In the **floor exercise,** men tumble across the floor three or four times in 50 to 70 seconds. Gymnasts perform moves that show strength, flexibility, and balance. They bounce high off the mat *(see Springy Floor, page 30)* and perform triple backflips and twisting double somersaults.

The **pommel horse** is a leather-covered horse with two handles (pommels) on top. Gymnasts use their arms to support themselves and swing their legs around the horse. Legs may whirl in circles like helicopter blades, or up, down, in, and out like scissors. Gymnasts swing around the horse while moving from one end to the other and back to the middle. Only the gymnast's hands may touch the horse.

Still rings are two wooden

Vitaly Scherbo won six gold medals at the 1992 Olympics.

rings that hang from cables 10 feet above the floor. Gymnasts hold the rings with their hands, swing in circles, and do flips. The athletes must show strength and steadiness, and do at least two handstands.

The men's **vault** is a five-foot-long horse that stands four feet off the floor. Gymnasts sprint down a runway, leap off a springboard, and dive toward the horse. They land on it with their hands, push off, and do twisting flips. Judges look for height, distance, and speed.

In the **parallel bars,** gymnasts swing between two evenly spaced rails. They do handstands and flips. Each gymnast must do at least one "release" move (let go of the bars in the middle of a trick, then catch the bars again).

The **horizontal bar** is also called the high bar. It's about nine feet high! Gymnasts swing around, fly into the air, do flips, and catch the bar again.

STARS TO WATCH

VITALY SCHERBO is one of the greatest gymnasts of all time. At the 1992 Olympics, he won six gold medals. Since 1991, he has won 12 world championship gold medals.

Vitaly grew up in Belarus. Until 1991, Belarus was part of the Soviet Union. The Soviet Union had the greatest gymnastics team in the world. The Soviet Union broke up in 1991. Vitaly competed for the Unified Team at the Olympics.

After the Games, Vitaly moved to the United States. He trains at Penn State University.

In 1994, Belarus beat Russia, which included many of Vitaly's former Soviet teammates.

"Wow," said Vitaly. "It was a great moment in my life."

ROUND-OFF

The round-off is a basic gymnastic move. Both men and women perform round-offs in their routines. The move allows a gymnast to run forward, turn around, and begin tumbling backward with power and speed. It is used in the floor exercise and balance beam events, and in some vaults.

High bar dismounts are exciting. Some gymnasts swing into the air and do three flips before landing on the floor.

No American male has ever won the all-around gold medal in the Olympics. That probably won't change in Atlanta. The world's best gymnast may be Vitaly Scherbo of Belarus (see Stars to Watch, page 27). Li Xiaoshuang of China won the all-around gold medal at the 1995 world championships.

Women

Although women started competing in the team event in 1928, a U.S. women's team didn't enter the Olympics until 1936. At that time, women competed separately in some events at men's competitions. At the 1952 Olympics, women's gymnastics was finally recognized as a separate sport with its own events.

In addition to team and all-around events, women compete in four individual events: vault, uneven bars, balance beam, and floor exercise.

In the **vault**, gymnasts sprint down a runway, jump off a springboard, and dive toward a vaulting horse. The horse is five feet long and four feet high. Gymnasts land on their hands, push off, and perform twisting flips. Many gymnasts perform a round-off onto the springboard and dive backward onto the horse.

In the women's vault, the

Legend

At the 1972 Olympics, a scrawny 17-year-old from the Soviet Union turned women's gymnastics upside down. **OLGA KORBUT** wasn't even expected to compete in the Games. When the Soviet team arrived in Munich, Germany, Olga was an alternate. She was called to compete when a teammate was injured.

Olga made the most of her chance. At 4' 11" and 84 pounds, she was smaller than most gymnasts. She spun quicker and flipped higher. She stunned the world when she became the first gymnast ever to perform a backflip on the balance beam.

Olga helped the Soviet Union win the team competition. She also won gold medals in the balance beam and floor exercise and a silver in the parallel bars.

Olga dazzled crowds with more than daring moves. She had charm and a smile that won millions of fans around the world. Olga was never the best gymnast in the world, but she was the most fun to watch. She inspired many girls to take up gymnastics.

OLGA KORBUT

SCORING

Because of a change in scoring, it's harder than ever for a gymnast to score a 10.

A gymnast begins with a maximum score in each event. Women begin with a 9.4. Men begin with 9.0. From these scores, judges take away points for mistakes, and add points for performing difficult tricks.

Tricks are divided into five levels of difficulty. An "A" trick is the easiest. An "E" is the most difficult. Most Olympic routines contain tricks from all five levels.

By doing extra "D" or "E" tricks, such as a triple back flip on the floor, a gymnast adds points. This way, gymnasts can still score a 10.

horse is turned sideways. Judges look for height, a straight body position (on the horse and in the air), and a solid landing.

The **uneven bars** are two wooden bars connected by cables or poles. The bars are at different heights, and the gymnasts swing over, under, and between the bars. The gymnasts swing in giant circles, bounce from one bar to the other, and let go of the bars to perform flips. They are always moving, using many grip changes, direction changes, releases, regrasps, and circle swings.

The **balance beam** is the most difficult of the women's events. The beam is 16 feet 3 inches long and four feet high, but it is only four inches wide. Gymnasts perform split leaps, back handsprings, full

U.S. fans have high hopes for 14-year-old Dominique Moceanu.

STARS TO WATCH

★ **DOMINIQUE MOCEANU**, the Number 1 gymnast in the U.S., is ready-made for show business. The 14-year-old was born in Hollywood, California. Crowds love her bubbly personality and energetic routines. She always looks as if she's having fun.

Dominique won the U.S. junior championship in 1994. In 1995, she won the all-around at the senior nationals and finished fifth in the all-around at the world championships.

Dominique now lives in Houston, Texas. Her parents are from Romania. They were gymnasts, too. Her coach is Bela Karolyi. He coached gold medal winners Nadia Comaneci (1976) and Mary Lou Retton (1984).

If Dominique really were in show business, her movie would end when she wins a gold medal at the 1996 Olympics.

twists, handstands, turns, and jumps. Athletes must cover the entire length of the beam.

The beam has springs in it to make it bouncier. Judges will be on the lookout for steady routines and high-flying dismounts such as double back somersaults. Points are deducted for missteps, falls, form breaks, wobbles, missing elements, and steps on dismounts.

The **floor exercise** is probably the most popular event. It combines acrobatic (tumbling) and gymnastic (dance) elements. Gymnasts perform to music, and routines are 70 to 90 seconds long. The floor is 40 feet long and 40 feet wide, and gymnasts must cover the whole area in three or four tumbling passes. Gymnasts perform triple twists and double-back somersaults with full twists. Gymnasts must include graceful dance moves such as split leaps and pirouettes.

Lavinia Milosovici of Romania sailed to third at the 1995 world championships.

SPRINGY FLOOR
What launches gymnasts into the air during floor exercises? Talent, muscle, and *springs!* Springs make the mat extra bouncy. On top of the springs are plywood, foam rubber, and carpeting.

FAST FACTS

- **Fredrich Ludwig Jahn, a German teacher, is known as the "father of modern gymnastics." He taught gymnastics to strengthen kids in his country, formed the first gymnasium, and invented the parallel bars, horizontal bar, balance beam, horse, and rings!**
- **Starting in the year 2000, gymnasts must be at least 16 years old to compete in the Olympics.**
- **Many gymnasts use chalk to keep their hands from getting slippery.**
- **Leotards, the bodysuits worn by gymnasts, got their name from Jean Leotard, who invented the trapeze in 1859.**

Lilia Podkopayeva of Ukraine is the 1995 world champion. She could win the gold. Svetlana Chorkina of Russia is also strong. She won the silver medal at the 1995 worlds. Lavinia Milosovici of Romania was third at the worlds.

Dominique Moceanu of the U.S. *(see Stars to Watch, page 29)* should challenge for a medal.

Shannon Miller of the United States hopes to show that she's not over the hill at age 18. She won two silver medals and three bronze medals at the 1992 Olympics. She also won the all-around event at the world championships in 1993 and 1994. She did not perform well in 1995, but she plans to lead the U.S. team in Atlanta.

— by Tess Reisgies

Rhythmic Gymnastics

Lots of Olympic athletes are expert ball handlers. But how good are they with ribbons? If a rhythmic gymnast wants to win an Olympic medal, she had better be an expert ribbon handler!

Rhythmic gymnastics is a mix of skips, rolls, spins, and leaps. It has only been an Olympic medal sport since 1984, but it is very popular. Rhythmic gymnastics was the second sport of the 1996 Olympics to sell out.

Women compete in two events: individual all-around and group.

In the individual event, athletes perform four routines. Each routine is performed to music and lasts 60 to 90 seconds. Athletes perform each routine with different pieces of equipment: rope, ribbon, ball, and clubs. Athletes roll on the mat, throw the objects into the air, and perform simple acrobatic moves. Gymnasts are not allowed to perform flips or other difficult stunts.

The group competition will be part of the Olympics for the first time in 1996. Five gymnasts perform together, using hoops, balls, and ribbons. Group routines run two to two and a half minutes.

Athletes perform their routines on a 40-foot-by-40-foot mat. An athlete must use the whole floor.

Russia and Bulgaria dominate rhythmic gymnastics. Bulgaria's Maria Petrova won the world championships in 1995. Ekaterina Serebrianskaya of Ukraine is the European champion, and she finished second at the worlds.

— *by Tess Reisgies*

Bulgaria's Maria Petrova was the world champion in 1995.

Fast Facts

- Rhythmic gymnastics is also known as rhythmic sport gymnastics. It dates back to 18th-century Europe, when people exercised using small hand-held equipment. (Some things never change!)
- The U.S. rhythmic group has spent the past 20 months learning how to work together as a team. They trained six to seven hours a day, ate meals, and even watched TV together. Now that's teamwork!

Stars to Watch

★ **JESSICA DAVIS** kissed a frog in 1995. She wasn't looking for a prince — she was looking for good luck. Jessica, who is the best rhythmic gymnast in the U.S., collects good-luck charms. Before each meet, she kisses one of them — the frog!

Jessica, 18, is a high school senior in San Anselmo, California. She trains 3½ hours a day. She won the all-around at the 1995 national championships, and she has represented the U.S. in three world championships. Jessica is so talented that she doesn't really need help from her good-luck frog!

Judo

The word *judo* means "gentleness" or "giving way" in Japanese. Judo is a sporting variation of jujitsu [joo-JIT-sue], which is used for self-defense. Judo was invented by Dr. Jigaro Kano, in Tokyo, Japan, in 1882.

Japan hosted the 1964 Olympics, so it was allowed to include a sport of its own choosing. It selected judo, although only for men. Women's judo became an Olympic sport in 1992.

Athletes use an opponent's weight and movements to throw him off-balance. Competitors try to end a match in a move or hold that results in an *ippon*, which wins the match. An *ippon* can be scored in several ways: by throwing an opponent to the mat, by securing a hold from which an opponent cannot break free for 30 seconds, or by a stranglehold or arm lock that forces an opponent to give up. If a match does not end with an *ippon*, a referee and two judges determine which player's throws and holds were better.

Competitors, called *judokas*, wear a white robe, called a *judogi* or *gi*. Matches last four minutes for women and five minutes for men. Men and women each compete in seven weight classes.

One of the top judokas is David Duillet of France. He won the over-95 kilogram (209 pounds) division at the 1995 world championships. Toshihiko Koga of Japan won the 1992 Olympics at 71 kilograms (156½ pounds) and the 1995 world championships at 78 kilograms (172 pounds).

— *by Erin Egan*

Japan's Toshihiko Koga (red belt) was the 1995 78-kilogram world champion.

Fast Facts

- All commands in a match are given by the referee in Japanese.
- After the Japanese team performed poorly in the 1972 Olympics, all of the team's trainers were fired.
- One of the most spectacular moves in judo is the **Koshiwaza**. One competitor grabs the other by the lapels of his *judogi* jacket, then turns and throws the opponent over his hip. The opponent lands on his back on the mat.

Stars to Watch

⭐ Everyone in Japan has heard of **RYOKO TAMURA**. She is a celebrity because she is the world's greatest judo competitor in the 48-kilogram (106 pounds) weight division.

Ryoko won a silver medal at the 1992 Olympics. She was only 16 years old! She then won gold medals at the world championships in 1993 and 1995.

Ryoko, now 20, is a student at Teikyo University, in Tokyo, Japan. She is nicknamed "Yawara-chan" after a Japanese cartoon character. When she is not practicing judo, Ryoko likes to go shopping or watch videos.

Last December, Ryoko won her 77th match in a row, but injured her knee. She should be healthy in time to become an international celebrity in Atlanta.

Modern Pentathlon

In 1912, modern pentathlon was introduced as a sport for men at the Olympic Games, in Stockholm, Sweden. Modern pentathlon (the prefix *penta* means "five") is a test of five skills required of a soldier of long ago: horseback riding, shooting, fencing, swimming, and running. Points are awarded based on the athlete's performance in each event. Thirty-two men will compete in:

◆ **Riding**: Athletes ride a horse over a 600-meter course with 15 jumps. The horses are picked at random, making this event one of the toughest. Athletes have 20 minutes to warm up with the horse.

◆ **Shooting**: Athletes use air pistols to fire pellets at a target 10 meters away. The target is six inches in diameter. Pentathletes take 20 shots. For each shot, a competitor has three seconds to raise his pistol, aim, and fire.

◆ **Fencing**: Each athlete faces every other competitor using the epée, or dueling sword. A competitor must touch his opponent with the tip of his sword within two minutes to win the match.

◆ **Swimming**: Athletes swim 300 meters freestyle in a pool. A time of 3 minutes 54 seconds earns points. For faster times, points are added; for slower times, points are deducted.

◆ **Running**: In this 4,000-meter cross-country run, competitors start according to their point totals in the first four events. The pentathlete with the most points starts first. The competitor with the next-highest point total is second, and so on. The first runner across the finish line wins the modern pentathlon.

This may be your last chance to see modern pentathlon at the Olympics. It

Russia's Dmitri Svatkovsky is tops.

may be dropped from future Games because it isn't popular outside of Europe.

— *by Erin Egan*

★ Stars to Watch ★

MIKE GOSTIGIAN, age 33, began to dream about the Olympics in 1972, when he watched swimmer Mark Spitz win seven gold medals.

Mike finally reached the Olympics, but not in swimming. In 1988 and 1992, he competed for the U.S. in modern pentathlon. He also will be in Atlanta for the 1996 Games. Mike is the top pentathlete in the U.S. and is Number 10 in the world.

Mike tried many sports while he was growing up. "I was never great in anything," says Mike. "But I was good in everything."

At 16, he heard about a sport in which he could be great — modern pentathlon. Mike tried it and was hooked. Now he is ready to strike gold.

Rowing

"Row, row, row your boat..." Wait! Forget that song. When you're trying to pull a 58-foot boat through a 1¼-mile course at 13 miles per hour, there's no way to row gently down the stream.

There are 14 rowing events in the Olympics, eight for men and six for women. The events are divided into two types: scull and sweep.

In the scull events, each rower pulls two oars, one with each hand. Men and women each compete in one-person, two-person, and four-person sculling events.

In the sweep events, each rower pulls one oar using both hands. Men compete in two-person, four-person, and eight-person sweep events. Women compete in two-person and eight-person events.

In two of the sweep events, an extra person, called a coxswain [COX-en], sits in the back of the boat and uses a rudder to steer. (In events without a coxswain, the rower nearest the front of the boat uses a foot pedal to steer.) The coxswain also yells instructions to the rowers. Since coxswains don't row, it helps if they are small and light.

ROWING BACKWARD

Unlike paddlers in canoe and kayak events, rowers face backward. Their oars are attached to the sides of the boat. Rowers pull the oars, rather than push them. The rower's feet are attached to a plate in the bottom of the boat. As the rower pulls with her arms, she pushes with her legs, forcing the seat to slide backward *(see illustration, below)*. All of this pulling and pushing generates a lot of power. It also helps make rowers among the best-conditioned athletes in the world.

The long, narrow boats used in rowing are called shells. Most are made of strong, lightweight materials such as kevlar, which also is used to make bulletproof vests. Boats range in length from 26 feet, for a single scull, to 58 feet, for an eight-rower shell.

The rowing competition at the 1996 Olympics will be held on Lake Lanier, in Gainesville, Georgia. The course is 2,000 meters (about 1¼ miles) long and is divided into six lanes. Rowers advance through preliminary heats. The crews with the six fastest times meet in the final. Each race begins with the bow, or front, of the shell touching a starting line. When the starting command is given, the rowers start pulling their oars like crazy.

Crews from Canada, Germany, France, Romania, and Ukraine are expected to do well.

The American men's and women's eight-rower

THE SLIDING SEAT
All shells and sculls have seats that slide back and forth. The seats help rowers generate power. Here's how: A rower attaches his feet to a plate on the floor of the shell. He pushes back with his legs as he pulls the oar through the water. As the rower straightens his legs, his seat slides back. This allows a rower to use his arm and leg muscles to power the boat.

teams are strong. U.S. women last won an Olympic gold medal in this event in 1984. The U.S. men haven't won an Olympic gold medal in the eights since 1964.

Lindsay Burns and Teresa Zarzeczny of the U.S. are favored in the women's lightweight double sculls. This is a new Olympic event. (In the three lightweight events, rowers must be lighter than a certain weight.)

Watch for Silken Laumann of Canada in the women's single sculls. In 1992, a few months before the Barcelona Olympics, a boat crashed into Silken's scull and injured her legs badly. Silken recovered to win the bronze medal at the

Britain's Steven Redgrave and Matthew Pinsent are a great pair.

Olympics! Silken won the silver medal at the 1995 world championships.

The top men's pair without coxswain is Steven Redgrave and Matthew Pinsent of Great Britain (see Stars to Watch).

At the 1992 Olympics, Australia won its first gold medal in the four-man coxless sweep event. The four rowers on the team became known as the "Oarsome Foursome"!

— by Bob Der

- **The youngest competitor in modern Olympic history was a coxswain who competed for France in 1900. The boy, whose name is not known, may have been as young as 7 when he helped France win a silver medal in the pairs-with-coxswain event.**
- **Women began competing in Olympic rowing events in 1976.**
- **The eight-man team from East Germany that won the gold medal at the 1976 Olympics included a butcher, a plumber, a gardener, a mechanic, and a student!**
- **At the 1924 Olympics, one member of the U.S. eight-man crew was a Yale University student named Ben Spock. Ben later became a world-famous doctor and expert on raising healthy babies!**

STARS TO WATCH

STEVEN REDGRAVE and **MATTHEW PINSENT** of Great Britain are known for their ability to sprint away from the competition in a race.

"We use this to remind the other pairs that we'll whack them whenever they come too close," Matthew says. "We hope it will depress them all the way to Atlanta."

Steven and Matthew have been beating back the competition ever since they first teamed up in 1990. The pair has won five world and Olympic titles. They won a gold medal in the pairs-without-coxswain event at the 1992 Olympics.

Steven also won Olympic gold medals without Matthew in 1984 and 1988. Steven is only the second athlete from Great Britain ever to win three Olympic gold medals in a row.

Away from the water, Matthew and Steven enjoy playing golf together. Matthew also likes to quiz his partner on trivia. What's Steven's favorite trivia topic? Past Olympic champions, of course!

Soccer

One great thing about the Olympic soccer competition in Atlanta is that it won't take place just in Atlanta! Fans will also be able to watch live Olympic soccer in Athens, Georgia, and in these other sites: Orlando and Miami, Florida; Birmingham, Alabama; and Washington, D.C. Sixteen men's teams will compete, and for the first time ever, eight women's teams will compete in the Olympics.

Even though soccer is the world's most popular sport, Olympic competition has always taken a back seat to the World Cup, the major international tournament. The World Cup is held every four years to determine the world's best national team.

In 1984, professional soccer players were allowed to compete in the Olympics for the first time. Starting in 1992, Olympic men's teams were restricted to players who were under the age of 23, although each team could have three exceptions (called wild-card players). This rule helps limit the number of World Cup stars who play in the Olympics.

Soccer began more than 2,300 years ago. The ancient Greeks played a kicking and throwing game called *episkyros*, and Romans played a similar game called *harpastum*. Early forms of soccer were quite violent.

Modern soccer began in England in the early 1800's, when it was introduced in schools. The first soccer rule book was written in 1862, and the London Football Association was formed in 1863 (soccer is called football in every country except the U.S. and Canada). British sailors played soccer wherever their ships docked, and they spread the game around the world. People in the U.S. began playing soccer in about 1820. By the end of the 1800's, it was popular throughout Europe and South America.

Soccer is played by two teams of 11 players each, including a goalie. The object is to get the ball into the other team's goal. A goal is worth 1 point. Attackers and defenders are all on the field at the same time.

Olympic soccer is played on a field about 115 yards long and 75 yards wide, which is slightly larger than an American football field. The goals at either end are eight feet high and 24 feet

Legend

Brazil's **ROMARIO** is one of the world's greatest soccer forwards.

At the 1988 Olympic Games, in Seoul, South Korea, 22-year-old Romario scored his team's only goal in the final against the Soviet Union. Brazil lost, 2–1, but Romario was the leading scorer of the tournament, with seven goals. Brazil won the silver medal.

After the Olympics, Romario played for pro teams in the Netherlands and in Spain. He was among the top scorers in the two teams' leagues. In 1993, Romario rejoined the Brazilian team for the 1994 World Cup tournament. In Brazil's seven World Cup games, Romario scored five goals and helped his team win the Cup.

Romario is stocky, and at just 5' 6" tall, he was the shortest man on Brazil's World Cup squad. But he is speedy and strong. He plows through defenders and frightens goalies with his powerful shooting.

Romario grew up in the slums of Rio de Janeiro, and he has called himself a "street cat." As a child, he washed car windshields for money and played soccer in the alleys. Today, his success on the field has made him a celebrity in Brazil.

ROMARIO

Fast Facts

- Soccer players run as many as 10 miles in one game.
- Soccer was called "association football" in England in the late 1800's. This was shortened to "assoc.," and then to "soccer," which is used in countries where NFL-style football is popular.
- Some 200 million kids around the world under age 18 play soccer. In the U.S., soccer is the third-most-popular sport among kids, after basketball and volleyball.

wide. There is a 60-by-18-foot area in front of the goal. Attacking players are not allowed to touch the goalie in this area unless the goalie has the ball and has both feet on the ground.

Goalies are the only players allowed to touch the ball with their hands during play (except for a throw-in, which takes place after the ball goes out-of-bounds). Players move the ball down the field by dribbling or passing. They can play the ball with their heads, chests, thighs, or feet.

Games are divided into 45-minute halves. There are no timeouts, but referees stop play when a player is injured, the ball goes out-of-bounds, or a player commits a foul.

Referees may issue warnings, in the form of yellow or red cards. A yellow card means a player has committed a serious foul, such as tripping an opponent, or has been a poor sport. After two yellow cards, a player is thrown out of the game. A red card is given to a player who commits a particularly bad foul or uses bad language. A red card means the player is kicked out of the game.

Teams tend to have different playing styles. Some teams favor passing and are more aggressive on offense; others focus mainly on defense, and they station more players in front of the goal to stop the other team from scoring.

Current women's world-champion Norway and runner-up Germany have the strongest teams. China and the United States are also medal contenders.

Mia Hamm of the U.S. knows how to win.

Men's teams from Argentina, Brazil, Spain, Germany, and Italy will all be in the hunt for medals.

— *by Tess Reisgies*

Stars to Watch

★ The U.S. women's team will be a strong contender for a medal. A major reason for that is forward **MIA HAMM**.

In 1995, Mia led the women's national team in goals and assists. She helped the team win the bronze medal at the world championships.

Mia, age 24, has a long history of winning. She led her high school to the Virginia state championship; she led her team at the University of North Carolina to four-straight NCAA championships; and she led the women's national team to its first-ever world title, in 1991.

Mia's father is an Air Force pilot, and her family moved often while she was growing up. She was born in Alabama and lived in Italy, Texas, and Virginia.

When Mia was 5, her mom wanted her to take ballet. But Mia wanted to play soccer instead. She joined an all-boys' team. Fortunately for the U.S. team, she has been playing ever since!

Shooting

Most Olympic athletes need either strength or speed. But shooters need to be calm and steady.

In Atlanta, men will compete in 10 events and women will shoot in five events:

◆ **Free Pistol:** Men shoot a .22-caliber pistol at a two-inch bull's-eye from 50 meters.

◆ **Rapid-Fire Pistol:** Men shoot at a four-inch bull's-eye from 25 meters. Shooters have four to eight seconds to aim and fire a .22-caliber pistol.

◆ **Running Target:** Men fire a .177-caliber rifle at a moving target 10 meters away.

◆ **Free Rifle Prone:** From a prone (lying) position, men fire 60 shots at a half-inch bull's-eye from 50 meters. A .22-caliber rifle is used.

Lance Bade is America's best shot in the trap and double-trap events.

◆ **Trap:** Men shoot at four-inch clay targets (called pigeons) thrown into the air 70 meters from the shooter. Competitors use shotguns and are allowed two shots per target.

◆ **Skeet:** One or two pigeons are released up to three seconds after the shooter (men only) calls for them. Targets are thrown into the air from three feet or 10 feet off the ground.

◆ **Sport Pistol:** Women stand 25 meters from the targets and use .22-caliber pistols. The event has precision and rapid-fire rounds.

In the *precision round*, competitors have six minutes to fire 30 shots at a two-inch-wide bull's-eye. In the *rapid-fire* round, competitors again fire 30 shots. Targets start sideways to the shooter. When the target turns, the shooter has three seconds to shoot at a four-inch-wide bull's-eye.

◆ **Air Rifle:** Men and women fire a .177-caliber rifle at a target 10 meters away. The bull's-eye is the size of a pinhead!

◆ **Air Pistol:** Men and women each try to hit a dime-sized bull's-eye from 10 meters. An air- or gas-powered .177-caliber pistol is used.

◆ **Three Position:** Competitors fire 22-caliber rifles at a bull's-eye about half an inch wide from 50 meters away. Men fire 40 shots from each of three positions: lying, kneeling, and standing. Women fire 20 shots from each position.

◆ **Double Trap:** This is a new Olympic event for men and for women. Targets are thrown two at a time.

The best shooters come from Germany, Bulgaria, Italy, and China.

— *by Bob Der*

Stars to Watch

At 17, **KIM RHODE** of El Monte, California, is the youngest member of the U.S. shooting team. Her specialty is the double trap, a new Olympic event. In 1995, she won the U.S. national championship.

"The Olympics have been a dream my whole life," says Kim. "I would like to compete in as many Olympics as I can."

Kim started shooting when she was 6 years old. She practices three or four hours every day. She has already traveled to Argentina, Korea, Greece, and Germany to compete.

Kim is a junior in high school and has three pets: Missy, a German shorthaired pointer; Iggy, an iguana lizard; and Fred, a gopher snake!

Team Handball

Team handball is not the game played by two people smacking a rubber ball against a wall with their hands. That's *handball*. Team handball is played by two teams of six players and a goalie. The sport looks like soccer, basketball, and water polo all thrown together in a high-speed blender.

Team handball is played on a floor slightly larger than a basketball court. Players sprint from one end to the other, trying to throw a leather ball into one of the soccer-like goals that stand at the ends of the court. A team scores a point each time it throws the ball into the net.

Players may dribble or pass the ball, or they may run three steps with it. A player may not hold the ball for more than three seconds. Shots must be taken from behind a semicircle six meters from the goal. Players are allowed to take a running start and jump across the line to fire 80-miles-per-hour shots.

Defensive players may use contact to "check" opponents, but they may not use their arms or legs to push, hold, trip, or hit other players. A player who commits a foul is suspended for two minutes.

Team handball was invented in Denmark in about 1900 to give track and field athletes a way to stay in shape in the winter. It was first played in the Olympics in 1936, and it returned in 1972 as a men's event. A women's Olympic tournament was first held in 1976.

Team handball is popular in Europe and Asia, but it is not widely played in the United States. France, Russia, Croatia, and Germany have strong men's teams. The strongest women's teams are from South Korea, Hungary, Norway, and Denmark.

— *by Tess Reisgies*

The powerful South Korean women won gold medals in 1988 and 1992.

Fast Facts

- Team handball referees work in pairs and are not allowed to change partners. If one referee can't work a game, his partner can't either.
- More than 4.2 million people play team handball in more than 123 countries around the world.
- The U.S. team handball team recruits from college football, basketball, soccer, track, baseball, and softball programs.

Stars to Watch

Back in 1988, **DARRICK HEATH** dreamed of playing in the National Basketball Association. At the time, Darrick played basketball for C.W. Post College, in Brookville, New York. He was 6' 4" tall, weighed 209 pounds, and had amazing jumping ability.

During Darrick's senior year, a local team handball coach convinced him that he had little hope of reaching the NBA. Then the coach talked Darrick into switching to handball. Darrick's basketball skills helped him learn the sport quickly, and he joined the U.S. national team in 1989.

Darrick, age 31, is now the best player on the U.S. team. He still dreams of the NBA. But playing in the Olympics will be a dream come true.

Softball

Fast-pitch softball will be one of the new Olympic sports in Atlanta, and it should be very popular — at least among host-country fans. That's because the U.S. has the best team in the world. The U.S. has won the past three world championships, in 1986, 1990, and 1994, and is 110–1 in international competition since 1986. The only prize missing for U.S. players is a first-ever Olympic gold medal. Softball will be played only by women in Atlanta.

Softball should also be popular in the Olympics because it is a compact version of baseball. In softball, the pitcher's rubber is 40 feet from home plate instead of 60 feet 6 inches, and the bases are 60 feet apart instead of 90 feet. The outfield fence is about 200 feet from the plate in centerfield, and a game lasts seven innings. The only part of softball that's not compact is the ball, which is 12 inches around.

Most of the attention at the Olympics will focus on the pitchers. And with good reason. Top fast-pitch softball pitchers are awesome. They not only throw 70-miles-per-hour fastballs, but they also try to fool batters by throwing riseballs, dropballs, and curveballs. Some even throw knuckleballs.

Because the pitchers are so powerful and the defenses so strong, teams do not score many runs. Offenses try to move runners around the bases with singles and doubles. Bunts and stolen bases are common. Home runs are not. The U.S. team is an exception to this rule. It has great pitchers *and* great hitters.

Eight teams will compete in the round-robin Olympic tournament. The teams are the United States, Australia, Japan, China, Chinese Taipei, Canada, Puerto Rico, and the Netherlands. All games will be played at Golden Park,

WINDMILL WINDUP

1. Begin with both feet on the pitching rubber and both hands on the ball at waist level. **2.** Lift both hands and the ball straight above your head. **3.** Bring both hands down in front of you, then swing your pitching arm straight behind you. **4.** Begin to step toward the plate with the leg opposite your pitching arm. Swing your pitching arm forward and up. **5.** Drive forward off your rear leg, and continue to swing your arm in a circle. **6.** Reach for the ground with your front foot. Pull your non-pitching arm down as your pitching arm swings toward your hip. **7.** Drive your weight forward as your front foot lands. Throw the ball with a snap of your wrist as the ball passes your hip. **8.** Follow through.

in Columbus, Georgia, which is about 100 miles from Atlanta.

Australia, China, and Japan could challenge the U.S. team. Australia will be led by pitcher Tanya Harding. In 1995, she came to the U.S. and pitched for the University of California at Los Angeles (UCLA). She helped the Bruins win the national college championship. She quit school and went back to Australia to join the national team as soon as the U.S. college softball season was over.

— *by Kara Yorio*

Fast Facts

- Women began playing fast-pitch softball in the 1930's. The first world championship was held in 1965.
- Fast-pitch softball is played by women in more than 40 countries around the world.
- The oldest member of the U.S. team is 34-year-old shortstop Dot Richardson. The youngest is 18-year-old pitcher Christa Williams.
- Softball was invented on Thanksgiving Day in 1887, in Chicago, Illinois. A man tossed a boxing glove to another man, and he hit the glove back to the pitcher with a pole.
- There are other types of softball — including slow-pitch and 16-inch. In slow-pitch, the ball must make a big arc before reaching the plate. In 16-inch, the ball is 16-inches around, and the players don't wear gloves!

Michele Smith of the U.S. is a hit at the plate *and* on the mound.

Stars to Watch

The message from the U.S. to the other teams at the Olympics is clear: Beware of left-handers named Michele. **MICHELE SMITH** and **MICHELE GRANGER** are the top pitchers on the U.S. team, and they are two of the best in the world.

Michele Granger, age 26, grew up in California. At the University of California at Berkeley, she set national college records for strikeouts in a career (1,640), season (484), and game (26). In one seven-inning game, she struck out all 21 batters. She joined the national team in 1986, when she was 16!

By the time Michele Smith got to Oklahoma State University, she could throw three pitches: fastball, riser, and curveball. In college, she learned to throw a dropball and a knuckleball. After she finishes playing softball, Michele, 29, plans to attend medical school and become a doctor.

The other members of the U.S. pitching staff are **LISA FERNANDEZ**, 25, **LORI HARRIGAN**, 25, and **CHRISTA WILLIAMS**, 18.

Swimming

At the first modern Olympics, in 1896, swimming races were held in a bay near Piraeus, Greece. Swimmers started each of the three races by diving from boats. The water temperature was 55 degrees, and the waves were 12 feet high.

In Atlanta, swimmers will compete in 32 events. They will swim races in freestyle, backstroke, breaststroke, butterfly, and individual medley (IM), in which swimmers use all four strokes.

The pool at Atlanta's Aquatic Center is 50 meters long, 25 meters wide, and three meters deep. It is divided into eight lanes. At the end of each lane is a touchpad. When a swimmer touches the pad, his or her time is recorded to one one hundredth of a second.

The talk around the pool in Atlanta could be about the use of illegal drugs called steroids. Steroids build muscles and help swimmers go faster. Chinese women dominated the 1992 Games and the 1994 world championships. In 1994, 11 Chinese swimmers tested positive for drugs.

Many Chinese swimmers have retired or are banned. But experts expect China's new swimmers to be fast.

Freestyle

Although freestyle swimmers are free to choose any stroke they want, they always use the crawl because it is the fastest stroke. The crawl was once called the Australian crawl, because it was popular in Australia in the late 1800's. Swimmers using the crawl look as if they are crawling through the water.

Freestyle swimmers lie face down in the water and move their arms overhead one at a time. To breathe, swimmers turn their heads to the side. Freestylers use what is called a flutter kick. Their legs move up and down one at a time like scissors.

In races longer than 50 meters, swimmers use a flip turn to switch direction at the walls. As they near the wall, swimmers do a forward flip and push off the wall with their feet.

Race strategies in swimming are similar to those in track and field. The sprint races (50 meters and 100 meters) require an all-out effort from start to finish. The

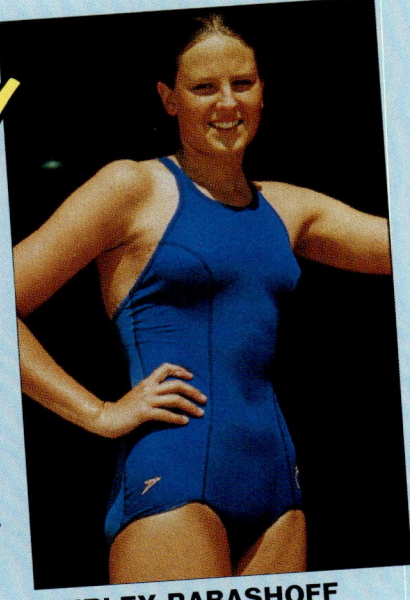

SHIRLEY BABASHOFF

At the 1976 Olympics, in Montreal, Quebec, Canada, freestyler **SHIRLEY BABASHOFF** of the U.S. won one gold medal and four silver medals.

Shirley was very disappointed. After her races, she said that the East German swimmers who had beaten her had used steroids. She noted that they were very muscular and had deep voices. People thought Shirley was being a poor sport. Her comments earned her the nickname "Surly Shirley."

Before the 1976 Olympics, women swimmers from East Germany had never won an Olympic gold medal. In Montreal, East Germans won 11 of 13 events!

As it turned out, Shirley was right. In 1991, East Germany and West Germany united into one country. Former East German coaches admitted that they had given steroids to their swimmers during the 1970's and 1980's.

"The whole thing was heartbreaking at the time," Shirley said in 1992. "But I've mended."

EVENTS

MEN	WOMEN
50 meters	50 meters
100 meters	100 meters
200 meters	200 meters
400 meters	400 meters
1,500 meters	800 meters

200-meter race is a controlled sprint. The pace is almost full speed. In the longer distances (400, 800, and 1,500 meters), swimmers must pace themselves. A swimmer who starts too fast may run out of steam and finish poorly. But if a swimmer starts too slowly, he or she may fall too far behind to catch up.

The world's best sprinter is Alexander Popov of Russia *(see Stars to Watch).*

Australia's Kieren Perkins holds the world record in the 400 and 1,500. In 1992, he won a silver medal in the 400 and a gold in the 1,500.

Chinese swimmers won both women's sprints in 1992. But China hasn't sent its top swimmers to any major meets since 1994, when 11 of its swimmers were caught using muscle-building drugs.

Amy Van Dyken holds the U.S. record in the 50 free. Teammate Jenny Thompson won a silver medal in the 100 free at the 1992 Olympics.

Franziska van Almsick, 18, of Germany holds the world record in the 200. She is a strong favorite in the 200 and 400 in Atlanta.

Janet Evans, 24, of the U.S. has been the queen of long distance swimming since 1988. But Brooke Bennett, 16, beat Janet to win the 400-meter and 800-meter events at the 1995 U.S. championships.

Alexander Popov of Russia is king of the freestyle sprint events.

FAST FACTS

- U.S. swimmers will be paid $50,000 by the sport's governing body for each gold medal they win at the 1996 Olympics.
- The water temperature of the Olympic pool must be between 78 and 80 degrees Fahrenheit.
- Alfred Hajos is the only man ever to win both the 100-meter and the long-distance freestyle events at the same Olympics. He did it in 1896. The distance race was 1,200 meters in 1896.

STARS TO WATCH

In 1990, Russian freestyle sprinter **ALEXANDER POPOV** was ranked 15th in the world — in the backstroke! That fall, his coach decided to switch the gangly 6' 6" swimmer to freestyle.

Alexander studied tapes of Matt Biondi, the 1988 U.S. Olympic champion. Two years later, at the 1992 Olympics, Alexander won both the 50-meter and 100-meter freestyle events.

Since the 1992 Olympics, Alexander, 24, has been nearly unbeatable in the sprints. In 1994, The Russian Rocket, as he is called, broke Matt Biondi's world record in the 100-meter freestyle.

Alexander began swimming at age 8 in Sverdlovsk, Russia. He now lives in Australia. He trains five hours a day, six or seven days a week. "When I am away from water for two days, I feel lazy and bad," he said. "When I get back in the water, it's like being born again."

Backstroke

The backstroke is an upside-down version of the freestyle. Backstrokers lie on their backs and lift their arms overhead, one at a time, to pull themselves along. Backstrokers use a flutter kick, and they can take a breath whenever they want because their faces are out of the water.

Backstroke is the only event that starts with the swimmers in the pool. Swimmers face the side of the pool and hold onto a bar positioned about a foot above the surface of the water. The swimmer's feet must be against the wall below the surface of the water, not curled over the edge of the pool. At the starting horn, the swimmers let go of the bar, push away from the wall, and dive backward into the water.

Backstrokers cannot see where they are going. They could easily bang headfirst into the concrete pool wall. To prevent unneccesary headaches, a line of colorful flags is hung across the pool five meters from each end. Swimmers know exactly how many strokes it takes to reach the wall once they pass under the flags.

Backstroke times have become faster due to a rule change and a new starting technique. Before 1991, backstrokers had to touch the wall with one hand before flipping around to push off with their feet and swim in the other direction. Now they can use a flip turn, similar to the turn used by freestyle swimmers. They turn before reaching the wall, and then push off the wall with their feet.

Backstrokers also used to come to the surface and begin swimming right away at the start. But they realized that times were faster when they remained underwater and dolphin kicked for a few yards before coming to the surface to begin swimming. (Swimmers dolphin-kick by kicking up and down with both legs at the same time.) Swimmers are faster

FAST FACTS

● At the 1988 Olympics, David Berkoff of the U.S. set a world record in the 100-meter backstroke. He swam the first 35 meters of the race underwater. David's start was called the Berkoff Blastoff. In 1993, a rule change forced swimmers to come to the surface within 15 meters of the start.

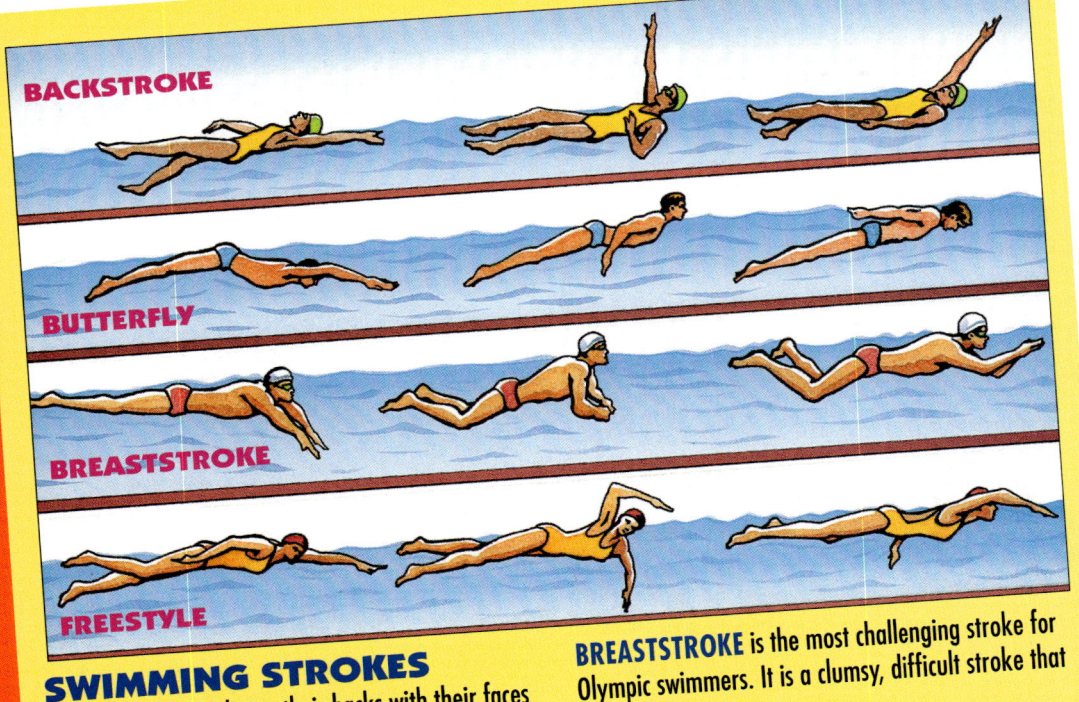

SWIMMING STROKES
BACKSTROKERS lie on their backs with their faces out of the water. They can't see where they are going.
BUTTERFLY is the most difficult stroke. It combines overhead arm movement with a powerful kick.
BREASTSTROKE is the most challenging stroke for Olympic swimmers. It is a clumsy, difficult stroke that is hard to learn.
FREESTYLE is the fastest stroke. When swum correctly, it also uses the least amount of energy.

Krisztina Egerszegi of Hungary, only 21, has already won backstroke gold medals at two Olympics.

underwater because there is less resistance. Backstrokers are allowed to stay underwater for 15 meters before they must come to the surface.

Jeff Rouse of the U.S. is the top 100-meter backstroker in the world. He won a silver medal at the 1992 Olympics. Martin Harris of Great Britain is ranked Number 2 in the 100.

Vladimir Selkov of Russia won the silver in the 100 at the 1992 Games and is favored in Atlanta. Martin Lopez-Zubero of Spain is the world-record holder in the 200. He won the 200 in 1992. He also won the 100 and was second in the 200 at the 1994 world championships.

Among the women, the fastest backstroker in the world is Krisztina Egerszegi of Hungary *(see Stars to Watch)*. She plans to skip the 100 in Atlanta, but she should win the 200. Barbara (B.J.) Bedford of the U.S. won the 100 and the 200 at the 1995 Pan American Games.

EVENTS

MEN	WOMEN
100 meters	100 meters
200 meters	200 meters

STARS TO WATCH

The 1996 Games will be the third Olympics for **KRISZTINA EGERSZEGI** of Hungary!

In 1988, at age 14, Krisztina won the 200-meter back to become the youngest swimmer to win an Olympic gold medal. Four years later, in 1992, she won Olympic gold medals in the 100 and 200 backstrokes and in the 400-meter individual medley.

Krisztina is a star in Hungary, where swimming is popular. When she's not training, she water-skis and rides horses. She has long fingernails, and she says they help grab the water.

Krisztina holds the world record in the 200 backstroke. She held the world record in the 100 from 1991 to 1994. In Atlanta, she plans to swim the 200 back and the 400 IM.

Why won't she swim the 100? "I'm too old now," she says.

Breaststroke

The breaststroke has been used by swimmers for hundreds of years. In the 1870's, Matthew Webb used the breaststroke to become the first man to swim across the English Channel. It was also the first stroke used in competitive swimming.

The breaststroke is popular with people who swim for fun, because it's easy and relaxing to do. Competitive swimmers have a different view: Breaststroke is not only the slowest stroke, it also is considered the most difficult stroke to master.

To begin the breaststroke, the swimmer floats in the water face down with both arms straight ahead and the hands almost touching. The hands and arms move away from each other, pulling down and outward. The arms may not be lifted above the water. The hands then pull in and up toward the chest.

This upward motion forces the upper body to rise, allowing the swimmer to raise her head and take a breath. When the hands are together under the swimmer's chest, the swimmer drops back underwater and pushes her hands back to the starting position. After gliding for a few yards, another stroke begins. During a cycle of one arm stroke and one leg kick, the swimmer's head must break the surface of the water.

While all of this arm movement is going on, the legs are busy, too. The kick that goes with the breaststroke is called the frog kick, because it looks like the kick that frogs use.

The kick begins with both legs fully extended and the toes pointed. The knees then bend as the heels come up toward the hips, just below the water's surface. When the feet are near the hips, the knees extend outward. The toes also point outward. Then, without stopping, the feet whip backward as the legs are

Fast Facts

- In the 1930's, an illegal breaststroke technique turned into the butterfly. In 1956, events for the butterfly stroke became part of the Olympics.
- In 1976, 12 of the 13 men's swimming events were won by U.S. swimmers. The only race the U.S. men did not win was the 200-meter breaststroke. That race was won by David Wilkie of Great Britain. He was the first British male to win a swimming medal in 68 years.

GOOD START
At the start of a freestyle, breaststroke, or butterfly race, swimmers stand on blocks, 30 inches above the water. They bend down and grab the front edge of the block. At the starting signal, they push off the blocks with both feet. Swimmers bend at the waist, place their heads between their arms and "punch a hole" in the water with their hands. They straighten their bodies and enter the water through that hole, splashing as little as possible.

EVENTS	
MEN	**WOMEN**
100 meters	100 meters
200 meters	200 meters

brought back together until the toes are pointing behind again.

Breaststrokers use an *open* turn. They must touch the end of the pool with both hands before turning to swim in the opposite direction. Swimmers keep their heads above the water to take an extra breath while making the turn.

Frederic deBurghgraeve [duh-BUKE-grah-vah] of Belgium is ranked Number 1 in the world in the men's 100-meter breaststroke. In 1995, he swam the fastest time of the year at the European Championships. He worked in a frozen-food factory until the fall of 1995. He now receives money to train full-time.

Norbert Rozsa of Hungary won the 100 and 200 at the 1992 Summer Olympics and is the 1994 world champion in both events. But he finished fourth in both events at the 1995 European Championships. Karoly Guttler, also of Hungary, is ranked Number 2 in the world in the 100 and third in the 200. Two Russians, Andrei Korneev and Andrei Ivanov, are strong in the 200.

Eric Wunderlich of the U.S. won the 100 and placed second in the 200 at the 1995 Pan Pacific Championships. At the 1994 world championships, he won the silver medal in the 200, just missing the gold.

Australian Samantha Riley was '94 World Swimmer of the Year.

Australians Samantha Riley and Rebecca Brown *(see Stars to Watch)* should do well at the 1996 Olympics. Samantha is the world-record holder in the 100; Rebecca holds the world record in the 200. Penelope Heyns swims for South Africa but attends the University of Nebraska. She set South African records in the 100 and 200 events at the 1995 Pan Pacific Championships. Amanda Beard of the U.S. could contend for a medal. Amanda won the 100-meter breaststroke and was second in the 200 at the 1995 USA Summer National Championships.

STARS TO WATCH

Australian swimmers **SAMANTHA RILEY** and **REBECCA BROWN** have a lot in common. Samantha, age 23, and Rebecca, 19, are both world-record holders in the breaststroke. They are both from Brisbane, Australia. Both also have asthma, a condition that makes breathing difficult, but which was helped by swimming.

In 1988, Samantha joined the Australian national team. She won a bronze medal in the 100-meters at the 1992 Olympics. In 1994, she became the first woman to win both the 100 meters and 200 meters at the world championships.

Rebecca started swimming when she was 12. Five years later, at the 1994 Australian championships, she broke the world record in the 200.

In Atlanta, these two plan to have gold medals in common.

Butterfly

The butterfly is the newest Olympic swimming stroke. It was added at the 1956 Olympic Games, in Melbourne, Australia.

Swimmers began using the butterfly stroke as early as the 1930's. It was a variation of the breaststroke. Swimmers found that they could swim faster if they lifted their arms out of the water at the end of each stroke to recover for the next stroke.

To begin the butterfly, swimmers lie facedown in the water with their arms straight ahead, as in the breaststroke. The swimmer pulls her arms outward, then deeper into the water, and then back toward her legs. At the end of the stroke, the swimmer's arms come out of the water and are thrown forward to the starting position. Swimmers' arms look like butterfly wings as they swing forward above the water. As the swimmer's arms come out of the water, the swimmer lifts her head and takes a breath.

The dolphin kick is used to help propel the swimmer along in the butterfly. In the dolphin kick, the legs don't alternate up and down; instead, the swimmer keeps both legs together and kicks them up and down at the same time, the way a dolphin moves its tail.

The kick is performed twice during each arm cycle. The first kick occurs as the swimmer's hands enter the water to begin the pull. The second kick takes place as the swimmer completes the stroke and lifts her head out of the water for a breath.

As in the breaststroke, butterfly swimmers use an open turn. They must touch the end of the pool with both hands before turning to swim in the opposite direction. Swimmers keep their heads above the water while making the turn.

World records could be broken in men's and women's butterfly events at the 1996 Olympics.

Denis Pankratov of Russia *(see Stars to Watch, page 49)* had an amazing year in 1995. He set the world record in the 100 fly at the European Championships. He also set the world record in the 200.

Scott Miller of Australia won both the 100 and 200

Fast Facts

- Michael Gross of Germany dominated butterfly events from 1981 to 1988. He stood 6' 7" tall. When he spread his arms, Michael had a wingspan of 7' 4"!
- In 1988, Anthony Nesty of Suriname (a small country off the coast of South America) won the gold medal in the 100-meter butterfly. It was the first gold medal an athlete from his country had ever won. He also was the first black swimmer to win an Olympic gold medal.

Legend

MARK SPITZ

Before the 1968 Olympics, **MARK SPITZ** predicted that he would win six gold medals. The pressure proved too much for him. He won two gold medals in the relays, but he won just one silver medal and one bronze in the individual events.

At the 1972 Games, Mark's first race was the 200-meter butterfly. Mark held the world record in the event, but he was still nervous. He had finished last in the final of the event in 1968. This time, he won easily, breaking his own world record.

Mark went on to become the first person in history to win seven gold medals in one Olympics. His other golds came in the 100 and 200 freestyle events, the 100 butterfly, the 4x100 and 4x200 freestyle relays, and the 4x100 medley relay.

No other Olympic swimmer had ever won more than five gold medals. Mark set world records in every event. His 100-meter butterfly world record stood for five years. He retired in 1973.

In 1990, he announced that he would try to make the 1992 Olympic team. Mark swam in exhibition matches, but he lost by such large margins that he retired again — this time for good.

SI FOR KIDS is cool. Because it's the magazine designed especially for boys and girls ages 8-14. Full of action-packed photos, great puzzles, and exciting writing that <u>make reading fun</u>.

Send for a full year (12 issues) for just $23.95. That's over 32% off the cover price.

Send SI FOR KIDS to:

___/___/___

Name   (please print)   Date of Birth

Address

City   State   Zip

Please bill: ☐ 12 issues ☐ 24 issues ☐ 36 issues

Name

Address

City   State   Zip

SKAD6G4

Check here if:
☐ Birthday gift
☐ Other gift

For Fastest Service, Call 1-800-826-0025

*Cover price is $2.95. SI FOR KIDS is published monthly except for an expanded issue in July 1996. Price $29.95 + QST & GST in Canada, $49.00 other foreign. Please allow 4-8 weeks for delivery of first issue. Prices valid through July 1, 1996.

5ISKBV

NO POSTAGE
NECESSARY
IF MAILED
IN THE
UNITED STATES

BUSINESS REPLY MAIL
FIRST-CLASS MAIL **PERMIT NO. 15** **BIRMINGHAM AL**

POSTAGE WILL BE PAID BY ADDRESSEE

PO BOX 830606
BIRMINGHAM AL 35282-9487

In 1995, Denis Pankratov of Russia broke the 100 fly world record, swimming's oldest men's record.

EVENTS	
MEN	**WOMEN**
100 meters	100 meters
200 meters	200 meters

fly events at the 1995 Pan Pacific Championships. He and teammate Scott Goodman (who call themselves "Dumb and Dumber") persuaded five other U.S. swimmers to shave their heads for the meet to show team spirit!

Don't count out Mel Stewart of the United States. Mel is a former world-record holder in the 200-meter fly, and he won the event at the 1992 Olympics. Mel's swimming style is different from other butterfly swimmers: He turns his head to breath to the side, more like a freestyle swimmer.

A long shot to win a medal is Sabir Muhammad, whose hometown is Atlanta. He was second in the 100 at the 1995 U.S. summer nationals. Sabir is one of the few black swimmers to represent the U.S. in international competition.

Susan O'Neill of Australia could break the two 15-year-old butterfly records held by Mary T. Meagher of the United States. Susan injured her shoulder in April 1995. But she recovered to win the 100 and 200 at the 1995 Pan Pacific Championships.

Jenny Thompson of the U.S. also could medal in the 100 butterfly. She won the event at the 1995 U.S. summer nationals. Summer Sanders of the U.S. won the 200 fly at the 1992 Olympics and may challenge for a medal in Atlanta. Summer retired from swimming in January 1994, but she decided to return to the pool 17 months later.

STARS TO WATCH

★ **DENIS PANKRATOV** was not nice to U.S. swimmers last summer. In June 1995, the blond butterfly specialist from Russia broke U.S. swimmer Mel Stewart's four-year-old 200-meter record by almost half a second. In August, Denis broke Pablo Morales's nine-year-old record in the 100 butterfly by more than half a second.

Denis, 22, is a student in Volgograd, Russia. He is the first swimmer since Germany's Michael Gross to hold world records in the 100 and 200 butterfly events at the same time.

Denis's trademark is his black bathing cap. He is one of many butterfly swimmers who uses the underwater start. Denis dives in and remains under the surface for an astounding 26 meters! He hopes this will help him surface with two gold medals in Atlanta.

Individual Medley

In music, a medley is a series of different songs. In swimming, the individual medley event is a series of all four swimming strokes.

The individual medley (IM) determines the best all-around swimmer. In the 200 IM, swimmers race one length of the pool (50 meters) using the butterfly, followed by a length each of backstroke, breaststroke, and freestyle. In the 400, swimmers race two lengths of the pool (100 meters) in each stroke. The 400 IM became an Olympic event in 1964; the 200 IM was added four years later.

Jani Sievinen of Finland is the top-ranked IM swimmer. He won the 200 and 400 IMs at the 1995 European Championships, and he swam the year's fastest times in the world in both events. He holds the world record in the 200.

Tom Dolan was named U.S. Swimmer of the Year in 1994 and '95.

Jani will be looking over his shoulder for Tom Dolan of the U.S. *(see Stars to Watch).* Some experts call Tom "the best all-around swimmer in the world." Tom won both the 200 IM and the 400 IM at the 1995 Pan Pacific Championships. He holds the world record in the 400 IM.

Another American to watch is Eric Namesnik. Eric's specialty is the 400 IM, which he won at the 1995 Pan American Games. He was a silver medalist at the 1992 Summer Olympics.

Krisztina Egerszegi of Hungary *(see Stars to Watch, page 45)* is the best woman 400 IM swimmer in the world. She won the gold medal in the event at the 1992 Summer Olympics.

Elli Overton of Australia was a surprise winner of the 200 IM at the 1995 Pan Pacific Championships. Her time was the fastest of the year.

U.S. swimmers Allison Wagner and Kristen Quance have a shot at medals in Atlanta. Allison was second in the 400

EVENTS

MEN	WOMEN
INDIVIDUAL MEDLEY	
200 meters	200 meters
400 meters	400 meters
RELAYS	
4x100 freestyle	4x100 freestyle
4x200 freestyle	4x200 freestyle
4x100 medley	4x100 medley

STARS TO WATCH

Swimmer **TOM DOLAN** has trouble breathing — and not just when he is underwater. His trachea [TRAY-kee-uh], the breathing passage in the throat, is smaller than it should be. He also has asthma, a condition that limits how much oxygen he can take in.

Still, Tom, age 20, is an amazing swimmer. He is the world-record holder and the world champion in the grueling 400-meter individual medley. Tom attends the University of Michigan. In March 1995, he set three U.S. records at the college swimming and diving championships, leading Michigan to its first championship in 34 years.

In his spare time, Tom listens to rap music and writes songs. His hobby is working as a disc jockey. His deejay nickname is MC Mass Confusion.

IM at the 1995 Pan Pacific Championships. At the 1994 world championships, she won silver medals in the 200 IM and 400 IM. Kristen was third in the 400 IM at the 1994 world championships and first in that event at the 1995 U.S. summer nationals.

Relays

The 1996 Olympics will be the first in which men *and* women will swim three relays — two freestyle and one medley. The 4x200-meter freestyle relay is the new event for women.

In the 4x100 and 4x200 freestyle relays, countries put their four fastest 100-meter or 200-meter freestyle swimmers together.

In the 4x100 medley relay, countries pick their fastest swimmers in each of the four strokes. The order of the medley relay is as follows: backstroke, breaststroke, butterfly, and freestyle.

Each swimmer swims either two lengths of the pool (100 meters) or four lengths (200 meters). One swimmer "hands off" to the next swimmer by touching the wall. The swimmer waiting on the blocks may not leave until her teammate has touched. The wall and the blocks have electronic sensors on them, and a light flips on if a swimmer takes off before her teammate touches the wall.

U.S. women have dominated the 4x100 freestyle relay event at the

FAST FACTS

● When he was 15, Tamás Darnyi of Hungary lost the vision in his left eye after he was hit by a snowball. In 1988, Tamás won gold medals in the 200 IM and the 400 IM, setting world records in both. He won both events again at the 1992 Games.

● The U.S. men have won the gold medal in the 4x100 freestyle relay each time the event has been included in the Olympics since 1964.

Olympics, and the U.S. is still strong. Relay teams from Australia, Japan, Germany, and, possibly, China, could also contend for medals.

The U.S. women are also the heavy favorite in the 4x200 relay.

The Australian women's 4x100 medley relay team swam 1995's fastest time, at the Pan Pacific Championships. The U.S., Japan, and Canada are also strong.

The favored U.S. men will look for competition from Russia and Australia in the 4x100 freestyle relay.

The men's 4x200 freestyle relay is up for grabs. Teams from Australia, the U.S., Germany, and Russia should be the ones to watch.

The U.S. men's 4x100 medley relay team swam 1995's fastest time in the world at the Pan Pacific Championships. Teams from Australia, Russia, Hungary, and Germany should make this race an exciting one.

— *by Erin Egan*

Legend

JOHNNY WEISSMULLER

If you watch old movies, you have probably seen **JOHNNY WEISSMULLER.** From 1932 to 1948, he starred in 12 movies as Tarzan, the Ape Man.

Before that, Johnny was one of the world's greatest swimmers. In the 1924 Olympics, he won the 100- and 400-meter freestyle events, anchored the record-setting U.S. 4x200-meter freestyle relay team, and helped the U.S. win a bronze medal in water polo. In the 1928 Games, he again won the 100-meter freestyle and anchored the winning relay team.

Johnny was born in Romania in 1904 and moved to the U.S. in 1908. In 1922, he became the first person to swim 100 meters freestyle in less than one minute. While he was training for the 1932 Olympics, Johnny was offered a job modeling swimsuits. Someone in Hollywood, California, saw his photo, and Johnny was invited to try out for the part of Tarzan. He won the role and retired from swimming.

Synchronized Swimming

If you turn on the television during the Olympics and see eight pairs of legs sticking out of the water, don't be alarmed. You have tuned in to synchronized swimming.

The word *synchronized* means "at the same time." In synchronized swimming, teams of eight women perform to music. The swimmers must be synchronized with one another and with the music.

Each team performs a 2-minute 50-second technical routine and a 5-minute free routine. All teams perform the same technical routine. It is worth 35 percent of a team's score.

In the free routine, teams perform their favorite, and most daring, moves. The swimmers may spiral headfirst into the water so that only their pointed toes jut above the surface. Or a team may build a pyramid, with one athlete standing on the shoulders of two of her teammates.

Seven judges score each team on creativity, difficulty of movements, and how well the swimmers on the team are synchronized.

The U.S. is favored in Atlanta. It has been ranked Number 1 in the world since 1991. The U.S. team is led by Becky Dyroen-Lancer (see *Stars to Watch*). Canada and Japan are also strong.

— *by Tess Reisgies*

The U.S. team "synchronizes" salutes and smiles.

Fast Facts

- Synchronized swimmers can hold their breath and stay underwater for more than a minute.
- Synchronized swimmers wear gelatin in their hair. Why? To keep their hair out of their faces when they come out of the water. Gelatin rinses out more easily than oil or gel.

Stars to Watch

★ **BECKY DYROEN-LANCER**, age 25, of San Jose, California, is considered one of the best synchronized swimmers in the history of the sport. In 1994, she won world championships in three events: solo, duet, and team.

Six days a week, Becky gets up at the crack of dawn to go to the pool for practice. She stretches, works on her choreography, lifts weights, and practices her routines. She goes home just before sunset.

Becky began synchronized swimming when she was 10. She trains so much because she usually competes in all three events. But only the team event will be part of the Olympics.

"I feel bad," says Becky. "But I really like working with a group. I think that's more exciting."

Water Polo

Question: What sport was so popular back in 1900 that it became the first team sport added to the Olympics?

Some hints: The sport was first played on rivers and lakes; it was played with a ball imported from India; the ball was called a *pulu*, which was pronounced polo.

The game, of course, was water polo. In Atlanta, teams of men from 12 countries will compete.

Water polo is played the way soccer would be played in a seven-foot-deep pool of water. Teams of six "field" players swim up and down the 33-meter-long pool, trying to throw a 10-inch ball past a goalie and into a 3-foot-high by 10-foot-wide net.

Players are not allowed to touch the walls or bottom of the pool. They may use only one hand to pass and shoot the ball. They dribble by swimming with the ball in front of them. With several hard "eggbeater" kicks, a player can rise out of the water to his waist to fire a shot at 50 or 60 miles per hour. Goals count 1 point.

Games are divided into seven-minute quarters. A team has 35 seconds to shoot, or it loses the ball.

Physical contact is common, but referees do call fouls. Minor fouls, called "ordinary" fouls, include touching the ball with two hands or taking the ball under water. They result in a free throw. A player committing a major foul, such as kicking or hitting, is sent to a penalty box for 20 seconds and the opposing team is awarded a free throw.

Hungary has won the most Olympic medals, with 12. But Italy, Russia, and the U.S. should battle for the medals in Atlanta. Spain is also strong.

— *by Tess Reisgies*

Chris Humbert is the big gun on the U.S. water polo team.

Fast Facts

- From 1912 to 1914, colleges could not compete in water polo because it was too rough.
- Early water polo players straddled wooden barrels floating in the water and slapped at the ball with kayak paddles!
- The U.S. is the only non-European nation ever to have won a medal in Olympic competition. It won a gold medal in 1904 and a silver in 1988.

Stars to Watch

Expect to see a lot of Big Bird in Atlanta, but this one doesn't live on *Sesame Street*. He's **CHRIS HUMBERT**, the star of the U.S. water polo team.

Chris is nicknamed Big Bird because he is 6' 6" tall, has a happy-go-lucky personality, and loves kids. Chris, 25, has played for the national team since 1989. He led the U.S. team in scoring at the 1992 Olympics. At the World Cup in 1995, Chris was the leading scorer among all teams. Many people say Chris is the best water polo player in the world.

Nevertheless, Chris's secret ambition is to play pro baseball! He is a left-handed pitcher with an 86 miles-per-hour fastball. When Chris's water polo career is finished, he hopes to get a minor league pitching tryout!

Diving

Diving is one of the most graceful sports in the Olympics. Divers perform somersaults and twists in the air before plunging into a pool.

Diving grew out of gymnastics in England in the 1800's. Like gymnasts, divers must be strong and flexible. Perfect timing and style are important in both sports.

Men and women compete in two Olympic diving events: springboard and platform. The springboard is flexible and gives divers a springy lift into the air. The springboard is three meters (9' 10") above the surface of the water. The platform is a solid deck. It is 20 feet long and 10 meters (about 33 feet) high.

Olympic diving competitions are divided into preliminary, semi-final, and final rounds. Only the top divers in each round advance to the next round. Men make 11 dives in the springboard preliminaries, 11 in the semi-finals, and 11 in the finals. Women make 10 dives in each round. In platform, men make 10 dives in each round; women make eight dives in each round.

Each diver performs a program that she chooses from six types of dives:

DIVE IN!
Divers use four positions: A **tuck** resembles a cannonball, with knees bent and legs close to the body. For a **pike**, the diver bends in half at the waist. In **straight** position, the body has no bends. **Free** is a combination of these positions.

◆ **Forward:** The diver faces the front of the board. Her head and body rotate forward as she dives.

◆ **Back:** The diver stands on the front edge of the board with her back to the water. Her head rotates backward, away from the board.

◆ **Reverse:** The diver faces the front of the board but her head rotates backward, toward the board.

◆ **Inward**: The diver stands with her back to the water. Her head rotates toward the board.

◆ **Twisting:** The diver twists her body forward, backward, inward, or in reverse as she dives.

◆ **Arm stand:** Platform divers may start from a handstand on the end of the board.

In the air, a diver uses one or more of the following positions: tuck, pike, and straight *(see illustration, left)*. A diver may also use the free position. This is a mix of one or more of the three positions. The most popular combination is straight and pike.

Dives are rated on their difficulty. For example, a simple forward tuck off the springboard is rated 1.4, while a backward 1½ somersault with 4½ twists has a 3.6

Sun Shuwei of China won the platform gold at the 1992 Games.

Fast Facts

- Divers are sometimes distracted by crowd noise or camera flashes. At the 1952 Olympics, divers were distracted by a photographer who was wearing a frogman suit in the pool.
- Patricia McCormick of the U.S. was the first diver to win springboard and platform gold medals at two different Olympics. She won her medals in 1952 and 1956. Patricia's daughter Kelly won a bronze medal in springboard at the 1988 Games.
- The youngest diver ever to win an Olympic gold medal is Marjorie Gestring of the United States. She was 13 years 9 months when she won the springboard event at the 1936 Olympics, in Berlin, Germany.

rating. The tougher the dive, the more points a diver scores if it's done well.

Seven judges give scores between 0 and 10 points per dive. The best and worst scores are tossed out and the others are added together. That total is multiplied by the dive's difficulty rating. The new total is multiplied by .6 to get the diver's final score.

Judges keep a sharp eye on the following parts of a dive:

◆ The diver's approach to the end of the board (about four steps) and her hop to begin her dive should be smooth and sure.

◆ The takeoff should be balanced and under control.

◆ The diver should spring high off the board. The higher a diver goes after takeoff, the more time she has to make her moves.

◆ The execution of the dive should be graceful and free of mistakes.

◆ The diver's entry into the water should be straight up and down with as little splash as possible.

China and Russia will have the strongest teams in

Stars to Watch

★ **FU MINGXIA** of China is only 17, but she's already made a huge splash in her sport.

At 12, Fu won the platform gold medal at the 1991 world championships. It made her the youngest person ever to win a major diving championship. In 1992, she became the second-youngest diver ever to win an Olympic gold medal.

Fu is tough to beat because she usually tries and hits the most difficult dives. Her spins and flips are tight and quick, and her entries into the water are almost perfect.

Fu started diving at 8. At 10, she was chosen to attend a special diving school in the city of Beijing. It was far from her home, so she saw her parents only twice a year.

When she's not diving, Fu enjoys math, reading, music, and eating ice cream.

Atlanta. China has dominated international diving since 1979. In the past three Olympics, Chinese divers have won 14 of 36 medals. They won three of the four gold medals in the Olympic events at the 1995 Diving World Cup.

The Chinese are well-trained and perform the hardest dives. Their best divers are Sun Shuwei of the men's team and Fu Mingxia of the women's squad *(see Stars to Watch, page 55)*. Both won gold medals in platform at the 1992 Olympics.

Russia is led by 1995 World Cup gold medalist Dmitri Sautin, the top male springboard diver in the world. Vera Ilyina won the bronze medal in the springboard at the 1995 World Cup.

The U.S. team has been in a slump lately. It has not won a medal in international competition since the 1992 Olympics. The U.S. failed to win medals in any events at the 1995 World Cup.

Three of America's best divers have been struggling. Defending Olympic springboard gold medalist Mark Lenzi may need surgery on his right shoulder. Mary Ellen Clark, the 1992 platform bronze medalist, has "vertigo," which means heights make her dizzy. Scott Donie, the 1992 platform silver medalist, has had trouble with his form and will probably compete in springboard instead.

If the best divers aren't healthy, the U.S. will hope for a surprise from Eileen Richetelli, the 1995 U.S. springboard champion, or from David Pichler, who was fourth in platform at the 1995 World Cup.

— *by John Rolfe*

China's Fu Mingxia spun to the gold in 1992.

Legend

GREG LOUGANIS

GREG LOUGANIS has been called the greatest diver of all time. He won five world championships and four Olympic gold medals. His story is full of triumph and tragedy.

Greg grew up in El Cajon, California. He was teased by classmates because he had trouble reading. Greg has dyslexia [dis-LEK-see-ah], which causes him to see letters backward or upside down. Other kids called him names because of his dark skin.

Greg found an escape in diving. When he was 8, he practiced diving in a pool in his backyard. At 16, he won a silver medal at the 1976 Olympics. In 1984, he won gold medals in springboard and platform. The last time a male diver had won both events in one Olympics was in 1928!

At the 1988 Olympics, Greg won the springboard gold medal after he hit his head on the board. He also won the platform event. Greg was the first male diver to win both events at back-to-back Olympics.

In 1995, Greg revealed that he had the HIV virus, which causes AIDS. Greg now teaches people who have the disease how they can live normal lives.

Table Tennis

The sounds of table-tennis balls *pinging* and *ponging* back and forth at the Olympics will be louder and faster — much faster — than you might expect. Table tennis at the Olympic level is a sport of speed and skill. The ball can travel at more than 100 miles per hour. Players must have great hand-eye coordination. Rallies usually last just four or five shots.

Games are played to 21 points (a player must win by 2 points). In singles, the winner of three out of five games wins the match. In doubles, a team must win two out of three games.

Both men and women compete in singles and doubles.

The best players are masters of spin. Different strokes create different spins and keep opponents guessing.

Another important part of table tennis is the serve. Good table-tennis players hide the way they're going to hit the ball until the last moment. This makes returning the serve much more difficult.

The white plastic ball is just over an inch in diameter. It is hit with a paddle that can be any size, shape, or weight, but the part that hits the ball — the blade — must be flat and hard.

The table measures nine feet long and five feet wide. It stands 30 inches off the floor. The net is six inches high.

Table tennis was invented in the late 1800's, but it didn't become an Olympic sport until 1988. Deng Yaping of China (see Stars to Watch) and teammate Qiao Hong are the top women's players in singles and doubles. Kong Linghui of China is the men's singles world champion.

— *by Kara Yorio*

Olympic table tennis is fast and intense.

Fast Facts

- Since table tennis became an Olympic sport, in 1988, China has won 11 medals and South Korea has won nine. The rest of the world has won eight!
- China won three out of four gold medals in 1992.
- Table tennis is the most popular racket sport in the world. It is played by more than 40 million people in 170 countries.

Stars to Watch

Bigger is not always better. China's **DENG YAPING** is only 4' 9" tall. But she has been the Number 1-ranked women's singles player for five years!

Deng's father was a champion table-tennis player. When Deng was 5, her father introduced her to the game. She was so small that she had to stand on her toes to see over the table.

Deng is an aggressive player, and she is quick, fast, and tricky. Deng, 23, works hard to be the best player in the world. She runs and plays table tennis every day.

Deng won gold medals in singles and in doubles at the 1992 Olympics, and she will compete in both events in Atlanta.

Deng's father taught her to "be second to no one in the world." For five years, she has been exactly that.

Tennis

If you're a tennis fan, get ready for some thrills. The best pros in the world will be battling for gold medals in Atlanta.

The Olympic tennis tournament has become one of the sport's major events. In 1988, Steffi Graf swept all four "Grand Slam" events (Wimbledon and the Australian, French, and U.S. Open tournaments) plus the Olympics to complete a "Golden Grand Slam." Gigi Fernandez, who won a gold medal in doubles in 1992, said that playing in the Olympics is more exciting than any other tournament.

Tennis is a fast sport. Serves rocket over the net at more than 100 miles per hour. Players have a split second to return a shot. Quick reflexes, stamina, and strategy are all important.

Tennis began to take shape in France about 500 years ago. The French played indoors. Players hit the ball over a net, off walls, and onto ledges that surrounded the court on three sides. In 1873, Major Walter Wingfield of England moved the game outdoors onto grass courts. He also made the rules simpler. By the late 1870's, tennis had taken off. Tennis clubs opened all over the world.

In the Olympics, men and women compete in singles and doubles events. In singles, one player competes against one other player. In doubles, teams of two compete against each other.

The goal in tennis is simple: Hit the ball over the net and onto your opponent's court one more time than your opponent does. When you do this, you win the point. A zero score is called "love." The first point is 15, the second 30, the third 40. The fourth point scored wins the game. A player needs a two-point margin to win a game.

The first player to win six games (with a two-game margin) wins the set. If the set is tied at six games each, a tie-breaker game is played. Women must win two out of three sets to win a match. Men must win three out of five sets in the singles and doubles gold medal matches.

Tennis was an Olympic sport from 1896 until 1924. The game was dropped from the Olympics because it was hard to tell the amateurs from the professionals. In 1988, tennis returned to the Olympics. All courts at the

Legend

HELEN WILLS

HELEN WILLS was one of the first superstars of tennis. From 1923 to 1938, she won seven U.S. national singles titles and eight Wimbledon championships. Only Martina Navratilova has topped that record at Wimbledon.

Helen changed the way women played tennis. Until she came along, many women stayed by the baseline at the back of the court and hit soft shots over the net. Helen was aggressive. She blasted hard shots, rushed the net, and ran all over the court, the way players do today. Even though she had a wild style, Helen's nickname was "Little Miss Poker Face" because she never showed emotion on the court.

Helen was 18 when she competed at the 1924 Olympics, in Paris, France. She won gold medals in singles, and in doubles with Hazel Wightman.

Helen got married in 1929, and she changed her name to Helen Wills Moody. She was elected to the International Tennis Hall of Fame in 1959. She was a star, but tennis did not make her rich. There was no pro tour during the days when Little Miss Poker Face ruled the court.

Fast Facts

- In tennis, love means "nothing." Love is used instead of zero when keeping score. The term probably comes from the French word for egg: "l'oeuf." Why? An egg looks a little like a zero.
- A tennis court is 78 feet long and is divided in half by the net. Singles courts are 27 feet wide. Doubles courts are 36 feet wide. There are three boxes in each half of the court. Players serve from the "backcourt," the rectangle box at the back. Serves must land in one of two boxes in the "service court" on the other side of the net.
- Before the 1960's, all tennis rackets were made of wood.

1996 Olympics will have a hard surface. (Tennis is played on grass, clay, or hard surfaces.) A hard surface is faster than clay, but slower than grass.

Sixty-four men and 64 women will compete in singles in Atlanta. In doubles, 32 men's teams and 32 women's teams will compete.

Countries such as the United States have a lot of good players to choose from. The hardest part of picking a team is choosing players who are strong in singles *and* doubles.

U.S. players will be selected based on the rankings of eligible pros. The men's team could include Pete Sampras, Andre Agassi, Michael Chang, Jim Courier, or Todd Martin. All are great singles players, but Pete Sampras and Jim Courier failed to win a doubles medal in 1992.

The U.S. women's squad will be chosen from a list that includes Mary Joe Fernandez, Monica Seles *(see Stars to Watch)*, Gigi Fernandez, Lindsay Davenport, and Chanda Rubin. Mary Joe Fernandez and Gigi Fernandez won the gold medal in doubles in 1992.

The U.S. women's team should win medals in both singles and doubles. The women will face strong competition from players such as Steffi Graf of Germany and Conchita Martinez and Arantxa Sanchez Vicario of Spain. The U.S. men will have to get past powerful players such as Boris Becker and Michael Stich of Germany and Stefan Edberg of Sweden.

— *by John Rolfe*

Monica Seles hopes to play in the Olympics.

Stars to Watch

In 1993, **MONICA SELES** was the best female tennis player in the world. But on April 30, 1993, a crazed fan stabbed her in the back at a tournament in Germany. Her wound healed, but she did not play pro tennis for more than two years.

In March 1991, Monica became the top-ranked woman player, a spot she held through 1993.

In 1995, she won 11 straight matches after returning to tennis. Her first loss came against Steffi Graf in the final round of the 1995 U.S. Open.

Is there anything Monica hasn't accomplished in the world of tennis? Yes . . . she has never played in the Olympics. "I want to be there in Atlanta," she said. "From what I hear, the opening ceremonies are a lot of fun. I want to be a part of it."

That's great news for the U.S. tennis team. Monica was born in the European country of Yugoslavia, but she became a U.S. citizen in 1994.

Track and Field

Track-and-field athletes are real-life super heroes. They run as fast as lightning, leap tall buildings, and are more powerful than bulldozers.

Well, maybe they can't do all of that, but they are pretty amazing.

Track and field is the oldest Olympic sport. In fact, the only event at the first Olympics, in 776 B.C., was a running race. That race was about 200 yards long. The winner of the race, and the first Olympic champion, was a Greek cook named Coroebus. He won a crown made of wild olive-tree branches.

At the 1996 Games, more than 2,000 track-and-field athletes will compete in 44 events. The marathon and the 50-kilometer walk will be held on the streets of Atlanta. The rest of the events will take place in Atlanta's Olympic Stadium. The competition begins on July 26.

Sprints

Sprint races are a lot like the races you run in school. Everyone lines up and runs as fast as he can for a short distance. The first person to cross the finish line wins.

Speed and quickness are the keys in sprint races. In the 100-meter dash, runners blast out of the starting blocks at the sound of the starting gun and build quickly to top speed. The 100 is over in about 10 seconds. Sprinters must get a good start if they hope to win a medal.

The winners of the 100 are known as the World's Fastest Man and the World's Fastest Woman.

Athletes in the 400-meter dash must run fast. But no one can run all-out for 400 meters, which is one lap around the track. The goal is to run *close* to top speed, but still be able to sprint to the finish. Races are over in about 43 to 50 seconds.

Hurdlers need to be fast, flexible, and strong. The 100-meter (women) and 110-meter (men) hurdlers sprint straight down the track while skimming over 10 hurdles. Women's hurdles are 33 inches tall and men's are 42 inches tall. The 400-meter hurdlers sprint once around the track while jumping 10 hurdles.

In relay races, teams pass a baton from one runner to the next. Each team has four runners. In the 4x100-meter relay, each runner sprints 100 meters before passing the baton. In the 4x400, each person runs 400 meters.

The baton is passed in an area called the passing zone,

FLEET FEET (AND WINGS)
If we staged a race between a sprinter and five fleet creatures, who would win? The spine-tailed swift would win (106 m.p.h.), followed by a cheetah (70 m.p.h.), jackrabbit (45 m.p.h), ostrich (30 m.p.h.), sprinter (27 m.p.h.), and butterfly (20 m.p.h.).

Michael Johnson's Olympic goal is gold in the 200 and 400.

EVENTS	
MEN	**WOMEN**
100 meters	100 meters
200 meters	200 meters
400 meters	400 meters
110-meter hurdles	100-meter hurdles
400-meter hurdles	400-meter hurdles
4x100-meter relay	4x100-meter relay
4x400-meter relay	4x400-meter relay

which is 20 meters long. If a team passes its baton outside the zone, it is disqualified.

The top contender in the 100-meter event is Canada's Donovan Bailey. He won the 1995 world championships.

Michael Johnson of the U.S. (see Stars to Watch) is the biggest star in sprinting. His specialties are the 200-meter and 400-meter events.

Frank Fredericks of Namibia won silver medals in the 100 and 200 at the 1992 Games. Butch Reynolds of the U.S. holds the 400 world record.

Top U.S. hurdlers include Allen Johnson, who won the 110-meter hurdles at the 1995 worlds, and Derrick Adkins, the world champion in the 400-meter hurdles.

The best men's relay teams are from the U.S., Canada, Jamaica, and Nigeria.

Among the women, Gwen Torrence of the U.S. should shine in the 100 and 200. Gwen is the defending champion in the 200. She has extra reason to do well in Atlanta: It's her hometown!

Defending Olympic champion Marie-Jose Perec of France is favored in the 400.

The U.S. has three of the top hurdlers. Gail Devers won the 100-meter race at the 1995 worlds. Kim Batten won the 400 hurdles and set a world record at the 1995 worlds, and Tonja Buford of the U.S. was second. Great Britain's Sally Gunnell won the 400 hurdles at the 1992 Games.

The top women's relay teams are from the U.S., Jamaica, Germany, and Russia.

Stars to Watch

MICHAEL JOHNSON, age 28, never planned on becoming the world's greatest sprinter. As a kid in Dallas, Texas, he was interested in school, not sports.

Michael was a decent runner in high school. But his goal at Baylor University was to earn a degree in business. He joined the track team to run relays.

Michael soon turned into an amazing individual runner. In 1995, he became the first person ever to win the 200- and 400-meter sprints at the world championships. In Atlanta, he hopes to become the first to win both races at the Olympics.

If Michael does this, he will be remembered as one of the greatest runners of all time. That's not bad for a bookworm!

Middle Distance

Sprinters get the glory and long-distance runners get the respect. But middle-distance runners deserve both. They must have great speed and amazing endurance.

Strategy is very important in middle-distance races. Runners circle the track between two times (in the 800 meters) and 12½ times (in the 5,000 meters). Races last from less than two minutes to more than 13 minutes. In all the races, runners must run fast enough so that they don't get left behind, but not too fast or their legs will turn into spaghetti.

Stars to Watch

Algeria's **NOUREDDINE MORCELI**, 26, is a master at smashing records. In the past four years, he has set world records in the 1,500 meters, 2,000 meters, 3,000 meters, and mile. His goal is to hold records for every distance from 800 meters to 10,000 meters.

Noureddine started running when he was a kid. He ran everywhere. He ran to school when he missed the bus. He ran along the beach near his home on the Mediterranean Sea. He even ran while he was fishing! If he got bored, Noureddine would stick his fishing pole in the ground and take off.

Noureddine ran his first race when he was 12. The race was four miles long. Noureddine was fourth. Ten years later, he broke the world record in the 1,500.

"I was always taught to move if you want to get something," says Noureddine. "Don't sit and wait."

Runners in all of the middle-distance races start in lanes. In all but the 800, runners cut to the inside of the track as quickly as they can. Runners in the 800 must stay in their lanes through the first turn.

The 1,500 is the Super Bowl of the middle-distance runs. It is known as the "Metric Mile." That's because 1,500 meters is just 120 yards less than a mile. Why is the 1,500 so popular? Probably because runners have always been fascinated by how fast they can run a mile.

The steeplechase is one of the most grueling of all track races. The race is slightly less than two miles long, but athletes must jump over 28 hurdles and seven water jumps. At each water jump, a 36-inch hurdle stands in front of a pool of water. The pool is 12 feet long and up to 27½ inches deep. Runners step on top of the hurdle with one foot, land in the water with the other foot, and then take a giant step onto dry land.

The middle-distance and long-distance runs are relatively new Olympic events for women. At the 1928 Games, in

Legend

In the 1960's and 1970's, boys in Kenya wanted to grow up to be **KIP KEINO**. Kip was the greatest athlete in this African country. At the 1968 Olympics, in Mexico City, Mexico, Kip had a bad stomachache. Despite the pain, he won a gold medal in the 1,500-meter event and a silver in the 5,000. At the 1972 Olympics, in Munich, Germany, Kip won the 3,000-meter steeplechase and the silver medal in the 1,500.

Kip ran with a long, easy stride. Often, he wore an orange cap pulled down around his ears. As he neared the finish line, Kip would fling off his cap and sprint to the finish line.

Because of Kip's success, running became very popular in Kenya. Today, many of the world's greatest middle-distance and long-distance runners are from Kenya.

Kip is not only a great runner. He is also a great person. Kip and his wife, Phyllis, opened their home in Kenya to more than 100 orphan kids. "They are all my children," Kip once said.

KIP KEINO

Algeria's Hassiba Boulmerka *(photo left, in green)* and Noureddine Morceli *(right)* rule the 1,500.

Amsterdam, Holland, several women collapsed after the 800-meter race. Officials thought women were too weak to race farther than 200 meters, so women's distance races were dropped from the Olympics. It wasn't until 1972 that a women's 1,500-meter event was added to the Games. In Atlanta, women will run every race that men run except the steeplechase.

Runners from Kenya are always strong in the 800-meter event. Wilson Kipketer grew up in Kenya, but he may race for Denmark, where he lives. He won the 1995 world championship and will be among the favorites in Atlanta.

The best 1,500-meter runner in the world is Algeria's Noureddine Morceli *(see Stars to Watch, page 62)*. Steve Holman is America's best hope in the event. Mel Sheppard was the last U.S. runner to win an Olympic gold medal in the 1,500. He won in 1908!

Haile Gebrselassie of Ethiopia holds the world record in the 5,000. But he may run the 10,000 in Atlanta. Moses Kiptanui of Kenya is the world-record-holder in the steeplechase.

In the women's events, Ana Quirot of Cuba is an emotional favorite to win the 800. Ana won the bronze medal at the 1992 Olympics. In 1993, she nearly died in a fire at her home in Havana, Cuba. In 1995, with her face and body still covered with scars, she won the 800 at the worlds. Ana's top competitor in Atlanta will be Maria Mutola of Mozambique. Maria has run the world's fastest 800-meter times each year since 1993.

Algeria's Hassiba Boulmerka won the 1992 Olympic gold medal in the 1,500 and is a two-time world champion. Hassiba is Algeria's first track and field Olympic champion.

Sonia O'Sullivan of Ireland won the 5,000 at the 1995 worlds. She went to Villanova University in the U.S., and now trains in England with male runners from Kenya.

FAST FACTS

- Kenyan runners have won the steeplechase in each of the past three Olympics. In 1992, Kenyans finished first, second, and third.
- The 5,000-meter race is a new Olympic event for women. It replaces the 3,000, which women ran from 1984 to 1992.
- Finland's Paavo Nurmi was probably the greatest middle-distance runner ever. Paavo was nicknamed the Flying Finn. He competed in the 1920, 1924, and 1928 Olympics. He won nine gold medals and three silver medals!

EVENTS

MEN	WOMEN
800 meters	800 meters
1,500 meters	1,500 meters
3,000-meter steeplechase	5,000 meters
5,000 meters	

Legend

EMIL ZATOPEK

EMIL ZATOPEK of Czechoslovakia looked horrible when he raced. His face was bright red. His tongue hung out of his mouth, and he groaned and gasped. Sportswriters called him Emil the Terrible because he was such a sad, scary sight crossing the finish line. But Emil had a secret. His pain and agony were an act. Emil wasn't terrible at all; he was terrific!

Emil competed in three Olympics. At the 1948 Games, he won gold in the 10,000 meters and silver in the 5,000 meters. At the 1952 Games, Emil won gold medals in three events: the 5,000, 10,000, and marathon. He is the only runner to win all three races in the same Olympics.

Emil's first marathon was the Olympic race in 1952. Fifteen miles into the race, Emil was in the lead with runners from Sweden and Great Britain. "Excuse me," Emil said to the British runner. "I haven't run a marathon before, but don't you think we ought to go a bit faster?" A few miles later, the British runner quit. Emil won by more than two minutes.

Emil returned to the Olympics in 1956 and finished sixth in the marathon. "At the Olympics you can say, 'These men are the best,'" Emil once said. "It is a big truth."

Long Distance

First, imagine running 26 miles 385 yards. Now imagine running that far in muggy, 100-degree heat!

Hot, brutal conditions await the marathoners and all the long-distance runners at the 1996 Olympics. The runners who can best cope with the heat will win the medals.

To help get ready to race in Atlanta, runners will train in hot weather before the Games. During races, runners will drink plenty of water and run at a slightly slower pace. The runners know they cannot win a medal unless they reach the finish line.

The 10,000 (6.2 miles) is a 25-lap race around the 400-meter track. To run fast for this distance, runners must be smooth and efficient. They bend their knees slightly and barely move their arms. They run with short strides and land softly on their feet.

Strategy is very important. Top runners may try to break away with sudden bursts of speed. Or, perhaps, one or two runners will set a hard, steady pace that wilts the rest of the field. If the runners stay together, the final lap will be a mad, furious sprint.

Fast Facts

- Women were not permitted to run the marathon in the Olympics until 1984. Joan Benoit of the U.S. won the first gold medal. The women's 10,000 was added in 1988.
- Until the 1908 Olympics, in London, England, a marathon was 25 to 26 miles long. But the royal family wanted to watch the start of the 1908 race. So the start was moved to the lawn in front of Windsor Castle. The finish line at the Olympic stadium was 26 miles 385 yards away. That has been the length of the marathon ever since.

The marathon is the longest Olympic running race. The race starts in Atlanta's Olympic Stadium, then heads into the streets of Atlanta. The race ends back inside the Olympic Stadium.

As in the 10,000, the runners in the marathon must use their heads as well as their legs. Some runners may try to burst ahead for a short distance, then cruise. Others will stick close to the pack and try to break away with a burst of speed when the race is almost over.

Walkers are known for their

EVENTS

MEN	WOMEN
10,000 meters	10,000 meters
Marathon	Marathon
20-kilometer walk	10-kilometer walk
50-kilometer walk	

wobbling stride. They walk this way because they must follow strict rules. Walkers must have one foot or the other on the ground at all times, and the leg that is on the ground must be straight.

Ethiopia's Haile Gebrselassie is the world's best 10,000-meter runner. He won the event at the 1995 worlds, and he holds the world record.

Predicting the winner in the men's marathon is difficult. Any one of at least 10 men are fast enough and smart enough to win. Mexico, Kenya, Japan, and Korea all have great marathon runners.

Valentin Kononen of Finland is the world champion in the 50-kilometer (31 miles) walk. Italy's Michele Didoni won the 1995 world championship in the 20-kilometer (12.4 miles) event.

Among the women, watch for Ethiopia's Derartu Tulu (see Stars to Watch). Portugal's Fernanda Ribeiro is the 1995 world champion. Lynn Jennings of the U.S. is a two-time Olympian. She won the bronze medal at the 1992 Games.

The women's marathon may be a battle between Uta Pippig of Germany and Portugal's Manuela Machado. Uta won the New York City Marathon in 1993 and the Boston Marathon in 1994 and 1995. She may run the 10,000 in Atlanta. Manuela won the 1995 world championship.

Russia's Irina Stankina and Finland's Sari Essayah should battle in the 10-kilometer walk. Irina is the 1995 world champion. Sari finished fourth at the 1992 Games.

Derartu Tulu outpaced Elana Meyer at the 1992 Olympics.

STARS TO WATCH

DERARTU TULU of Ethiopia won the 10,000-meter event at the 1992 Olympics. She is the first black African woman to win an Olympic gold medal.

Derartu finished 5.73 seconds ahead of Elana Meyer of South Africa. Until 1991, Derartu was not allowed to race Elana. That's because Elana's country kept white and black people separated. This was called apartheid. South Africa was banned from the Olympics from 1964 until 1991, when their country ended apartheid. Elana, who is white, was thrilled that she finally could race athletes such as Derartu.

After the race, Derartu and Elana hugged, and then they ran a victory lap together.

Jumps

Everyone knows that people can't fly, but Olympic jumpers come close.

Sergei Bubka of Ukraine is the world's best pole vaulter. He can soar more than 20 feet into the air! High jumpers don't use poles, but some can leap higher than eight feet. Ivan Pedroso of Cuba can fly more than 28 feet in the long jump. And some triple jumpers can cover 50 feet!

Men's jumping events have been part of every Modern Olympics. In 1928, the high jump became the first jumping event for women.

The women's long jump was added in 1948. In Atlanta, women will compete in the triple jump for the first time.

Athletes in the jumping events compete one at a time. Long jumpers start by sprinting about 50 yards down a runway. On their last step, they use one foot to spring from a take-off board. They land in a pit filled with sand. The distance between the far edge of the take-off board and the nearest mark left in the sand is the length of the jump.

Triple jumpers also begin with a running start. They leap off one foot and land on the same foot, take a giant step onto the opposite foot, and jump into a sand pit.

In the high jump, athletes jump off one foot and try to clear a bar that is balanced between two supports. A jumper keeps jumping until he or she misses three times at one height.

Pole vaulters use a fiberglass pole to clear a bar (see illustration at left). A vaulter jumps until he fails three times to clear a height.

In Atlanta, the competition in the long jump should be tight. Ivan Pedroso of Cuba won the 1995 world championship. Mike Powell of the U.S. holds the world record of 29' 4½". Carl Lewis of the U.S. has won the long jump at the past three Olympics.

Jonathan Edwards of Great Britain broke the triple jump world record three times in 1995.

EVENTS	
MEN	**WOMEN**
High Jump	High Jump
Long Jump	Long Jump
Triple Jump	Triple Jump
Pole Vault	

UP, UP, AND AWAY!
After sprinting down a runway, a pole vaulter jams the end of his 16-foot pole into into a "box." The vaulter's speed and body weight make the pole bend. As the pole begins to straighten, the vaulter swings and lifts his body until it is above the pole. The pole then flings the vaulter up and over the bar. Many vaulters practice gymnastics to learn to swing upside down.

Javier Sotomayor of Cuba leaped 7' 8" to win the 1992 Olympic gold medal in the high jump.

Mike Conley of the U.S. won the silver medal at the 1984 Olympics and the gold medal at the 1992 Games.

Cuba's Javier Sotomayor won the 1992 Olympic gold medal in the high jump. He holds the world record of 8' ½".

Sergei Bubka (see Stars to Watch) has been the world's best pole vaulter for the past 11 years.

In the women's events, Heike Drechsler of Germany is a long-jump favorite. She won the gold medal at the 1992 Olympics. Fiona May of Italy won the 1995 world championships.

Inga Babakova of Ukraine was the most consistent high jumper in 1995. But Stefka Kostadinova of Bulgaria won the 1995 world championship.

Stefka also won a silver medal in the event at the 1988 Olympics.

Inessa Kravets of Ukraine won the 1995 triple-jump world championship. She's the first woman ever to jump more than 50 feet. Ana Biruyukova of Russia beat Inessa seven times in 1995.

Stars to Watch

When **SERGEI BUBKA** was a kid in Ukraine, he was always falling into trouble. When he was 4, he fell into a barrel of water and nearly drowned. He also fell out of a tree, but was saved when his suspenders caught a branch.

Sergei no longer falls; he jumps! In the past 11 years, Sergei has broken the world pole-vaulting record 30 times. In 1991, he became the first vaulter to clear 20 feet.

Sergei won the Olympic gold medal in 1988. In 1992, he missed the opening height and was eliminated in the first round.

Sergei can do frontflips, backflips, and cartwheels! He is an all-around athlete, and does gymnastics to stay that way.

Fast Facts

- American Dick Fosbury invented the flop technique in high jumping. Dick would throw himself over the bar headfirst with his face up. Before the "Fosbury Flop," most jumpers rolled over the bar with their faces down.
- At the 1968 Olympics, Bob Beamon shocked the world by jumping 29' 2½" in the long jump. He broke the world record by almost two feet!

Throws

A long time ago, a strong arm and good aim were useful when it came time to hunt for dinner. That's because people hunted with rocks and spears. After dinner, they held contests to see how far they could throw their weapons. Today, throwing events are still a test of an athlete's strength.

The discus is a flat, saucer-shaped disc made of wood and metal. The men's discus is about nine inches in diameter and weighs about 4½ pounds. The women's discus is about seven inches across and weighs about 2 pounds. Athletes throw the discus from an eight-foot circle. If the thrower steps outside of the circle, the throw doesn't count.

Stars to Watch

JOHN GODINA of the U.S. became a star in 1995. In June, he won the national college championship in both the shot put and the discus.

In August, John won the gold medal in the shot put at the track-and-field world championships. The worlds were John's first international meet.

John also won 14 of the 15 shot-put events he entered in 1995. He had the five longest puts in the world for the year.

John grew up in Cheyenne, Wyoming. In grade school, he threw the discus. But when he got to high school, he was asked to try the shot put, too.

"I didn't like the shot put at first," John says. "It was hard to do and I didn't like the fact that I couldn't get it right away. It took me about two years to get to the point where I actually looked like a shot-putter."

Right now, John looks like a *champion* shot-putter.

Throwers hold the discus flat against their hand and forearm, with their fingertips curled around the edge. A thrower spins around 1½ times while swinging the discus with a straight arm as he turns. Using strength and the momentum from the spin, throwers can hurl the discus more than 200 feet.

Shot-putters throw a brass or iron ball from above shoulder-level. Athletes are not allowed to step outside the seven-foot throwing circle. The men's shot put weighs 16 pounds, and the women's weighs 8 pounds 13 ounces.

A shot-putter starts a throw from the back of the circle. He turns his back toward the throwing area and holds the ball beneath his chin with one hand. The athlete bends forward, then hops backward across the circle on one leg. On the second hop, the athlete turns and puts *(pushes)* the shot.

Most shot-putters use this backward hopping style, but a few use a spinning technique.

A javelin is a steel-tipped wood or metal shaft. The men's javelin weighs about 1¾ pounds and is about 8½ feet

Legend

BABE DIDRIKSON

BABE DIDRIKSON made an announcement when she arrived in Los Angeles, California, for the 1932 Olympics: "I am out to beat everybody in sight," said Babe, then 18 years old.

A few weeks earlier, Babe had entered eight events at the U.S. Olympic Trials. She won six and set three world records!

Olympic rules allowed Babe to enter just three events. She won gold medals in the javelin and 80-meter hurdles, and a silver in the high jump. After the Olympics, she became an outstanding golfer, baseball and basketball player, and swimmer. Babe got married in 1938 and changed her name to Babe Didrikson Zaharias.

In 1950, sports writers voted Babe the greatest female athlete of the first half of the 20th century. Even after Babe died of cancer, in 1956, her success inspired many female athletes — including a young girl in East St. Louis, Illinois. That girl's name was Jackie Joyner, who is now an Olympic legend better known as Jackie Joyner-Kersee *(see Stars to Watch, page 71).*

EVENTS	
MEN	**WOMEN**
Shot Put	Shot Put
Discus	Discus
Hammer	Javelin
Javelin	

long. The women's javelin weighs about 1½ pounds and is about 7½ feet long.

Javelin athletes begin by sprinting down a 40-yard runway. Just before reaching the foul line, they plant their front foot and throw the javelin from above shoulder-level. The tip of the javelin must break the surface of the ground when it lands.

The design of the javelin changed several times from the 1960's until the mid-1980's. As javelins changed, they flew farther and farther. From 1976 until 1986, the men's world record increased more than 35 feet, to 343 feet. In 1986, a new rule changed the shape of the javelin, limiting how far it would fly. In 1995, the best throws were back in the 300-foot range.

The hammer is a 16-pound metal ball that's attached to a handle by a four-foot-long steel wire. The thrower uses both hands to swing the hammer in circles, so it passes below his knees and above his head. After several turns, he lets go, sending the hammer flying about 260 feet.

Lars Riedel of Germany is a three-time world champion in the discus.

John Godina of the U.S. *(see Stars to Watch)* is favored in the shot put. John could become the second straight U.S. Olympic shot put champion.

Andrei Abduvaliyev of Tajikistan hurled the hammer for gold in 1992.

The best javelin thrower in the world is Jan Zelezny of the Czech Republic. Jan won a silver medal at the 1988 Olympics and a gold at the 1992 Games.

Andrei Abduvaliyev is one of the favorites in the hammer throw. He won the 1992 Olympic gold medal and the 1995 world championship.

Among the women, Ellina Zvereva of Belarus will challenge Ilke Wyludda of Germany in the discus. Ellina is the world champion. Ilke had the longest throw of 1995.

Astrid Kumbernuss of Germany was the 1995 world champion in the shot put. She will be challenged by Huang Zhihong of China, who won a silver medal at the 1992 Olympics.

Natalya Shikolenko of Belarus was the 1995 world champion in the javelin. She will be challenged by Trine Hattestad of Norway.

FAST FACTS

- In ancient Greece, the winner of the discus throw was honored as the nation's greatest athlete.
- Al Oerter of the U.S. won gold medals in four straight Olympics, starting with the 1956 Games.
- Tiny chips flake off the shot put each time it is thrown. Extra chips are added after every throw to make sure the ball is the right weight.
- Women started competing in the Olympic discus throw in 1928. Four years later, the javelin throw was added. The women's shot put event was added in 1948.

Legend

JIM THORPE

JIM THORPE of the U.S. won gold medals in both the pentathlon and decathlon at the 1912 Olympics, in Stockholm, Sweden. His decathlon score stood as an Olympic record for 20 years!

After the pentathlon, King Gustav V of Sweden told Jim: "Sir, you are the greatest athlete in the world."

Jim replied, "Thanks, King."

Jim was born in 1888 on a farm near Prague, Oklahoma. His father was part Native American and part Irish. His mother was part Native American and part French.

A year after the Olympics, Jim was forced to return his gold medals. Olympic officials learned that in 1909 and 1910, Jim had played minor league baseball and was paid $25 a week. Earning money playing sports was against the Olympic rules of the time. Jim was crushed.

Jim played pro football from 1915 to 1928. In 1963, he was one of the first players inducted into the Pro Football Hall of Fame. But Jim always felt bad about losing his Olympic medals.

Finally, in 1983, 30 years after Jim's death, the International Olympic Committee changed its mind. Copies of Jim's Olympic gold medals were given to his family.

Fast Facts

- The words "decathlon," "heptathlon," and "pentathlon" all have Greek origins. In Greek, "deca" means 10, "hepta" means seven, and "penta" means five.
- Bob Mathias of the U.S. became the youngest Olympic track and field gold medalist ever when he won the decathlon in 1948, at age 17. He won again in 1952.
- In 1960, Rafer Johnson of the U.S. defeated his former college teammate, C.K. Yang of Taiwan, in the decathlon. Rafer was chosen to be the final torchbearer at the Opening Ceremony of the 1984 Olympics.

Multi-Events

The men's decathlon and women's heptathlon look as if they were dreamed up by a sports fan with a bad sense of humor.

Who else would combine the hardest sprints, jumps, throws, and endurance runs into one competition?

In the decathlon, athletes compete in 10 events in two days. On the first day, athletes compete in the 100-meter dash, long jump, shot put, high jump, and 400-meter dash. On the second day, they compete in the 110-meter hurdles, discus throw, pole vault, javelin throw, and 1,500-meter run.

The heptathlon is a two-day competition of seven events. Day 1: 100-meter hurdles, high jump, shot put, and 200-meter dash. Day 2: long jump, javelin throw, and 800-meter run.

The athletes who win these grueling events deserve the title World's Greatest Athlete.

Multi-event competitions were actually created in 708 B.C. That year, the first known pentathlon was held, in ancient Greece. The pentathlon combined five events: javelin throw, discus throw, long jump, wrestling, and a foot race.

The decathlon made its debut in the modern Olympics in 1904. That year, the event was called "The All-Around Championship." It could have been called "The *Crazy* All-Around Championship" because all of the events were held on the same day!

From 1964 to 1980, women competed in a pentathlon. In 1984, two events were added to make the heptathlon.

In both the decathlon and heptathlon, athletes earn points based on how well they do in each event. The points are figured out according to a special chart. The athlete who scores the most points in all of the events is the winner.

How do athletes prepare for

EVENTS	
MEN	WOMEN
Decathlon	Heptathlon

a competition that requires so many different skills? Most athletes try to become equally good in all of the events. Others try to become outstanding in a few events. That way, an athlete can balance average scores in some of the events with spectacular scores in his or her strongest events.

The world's best decathlete is America's Dan O'Brien. Dan holds the world record and has won the past three world championships. But Dan hasn't won an Olympic medal. Dan was the favorite going into the 1992 Olympics. But a bad day at the U.S. track and field trials ruined his chances.

At the trials, Dan had a big lead entering the second day of competition. In the eighth event, the pole vault, Dan failed to clear a height that should have been easy for him. He scored no points in the event, and he failed to make the U.S. team. He has been looking forward to the 1996 Olympics ever since.

In the heptathlon, Ghada Shouaa of Syria is the favorite. Ghada won the event at the 1995 world championships. If she wins in Atlanta, she will become her country's first-ever Olympic track-and-field champion.

The most dramatic competition in the heptathlon may take place between Jackie Joyner-Kersee of the U.S. *(see Stars to Watch)* and Heike Drechsler, 31, of Germany. Since 1983, Jackie and Heike

Dan O'Brien and Jackie Joyner-Kersee should give U.S. fans plenty to celebrate in Atlanta.

have been the two best long jumpers in the world. Off the field, they are close friends. "Jackie is my greatest motivation," Heike once said.

Jackie has won two Olympic gold medals in the heptathlon. Heike is a newcomer to the event. Both are thinking about entering the heptathlon in Atlanta. May the greatest athlete win.

— *by Bob Der*

STARS TO WATCH

⭐ **JACKIE JOYNER-KERSEE** of the U.S. is the greatest heptathlete ever. Jackie won a silver medal at the 1984 Olympics, and gold medals in 1988 and 1992. At the 1988 Games, Jackie scored a world-record 7,291 points. No other heptathlete has ever scored more than 7,204 points. Jackie also won the gold medal in 1988 and the silver medal in 1992 in the long jump.

Jackie grew up in East St. Louis, Illinois. She was a star in basketball, volleyball, and track. She played basketball and ran track at the University of California at Los Angeles (UCLA).

Jackie enjoys talking to kids, and she encourages them to play sports. "Don't be afraid to be different," Jackie tells them.

Volleyball

The objective of volleyball is simple: Two teams hit a ball over a net until one team misses. Sounds boring, right? *Wrong!* In Olympic volleyball, teams move from offense to defense and back to offense within seconds. Players dive to the floor, sprint into position, and jump three feet into the air to hit a 100-miles-per-hour spike! *Wow!*

Volleyball was never intended to be such a powerful, fast-paced sport. It was invented in 1895 by William Morgan, a YMCA instructor in Holyoke, Massachusetts. He created volleyball because he thought basketball was too fast for middle-age men.

Volleyball is played by two teams of six players each on a court 59 feet long and 29 feet 6 inches wide. The court is divided in half by a net. The net is 7' 11⅝" high for men and 7' 4⅛" high for women.

Players on each team try to hit the 10-inch ball over the net and into the opponent's court so that it can't be hit back. The serving team scores a point each time it hits an unreturnable shot. The team keeps serving until it fails to score. Only the serving team may score. The defensive team gains the serve, and a chance to score, when it hits an unreturnable ball. This is called a sideout.

The first team to score 15 points (with a 2-point margin) wins the game. A team must win three games to win a match.

Teams may hit the ball twice before they must whack it over the net. Hits may be made with a clinched fist or an open hand, but players are not allowed to scoop, lift, or push the ball.

Play begins when a player serves the ball from behind the end line. Players use a variety of serves:

◆ A ball hit with no spin is called a floater. It bobs up and down like a knuckleball in baseball.

◆ Some players throw the ball into the air, run forward, jump, and slam the ball as hard as they can. This is called a jump serve, and the ball can reach speeds of 80 miles per hour.

◆ A ball with a lot of top spin drops like a rock after it crosses the net. Defensive players must react quickly to reach the ball before it hits the floor.

The defensive team now sets up its attack. One player fields the serve by

Legend

FLO HYMAN

FLO HYMAN'S dream almost came true at the 1984 Olympics. Flo had joined the U.S. team in 1974 because she wanted to compete in the 1980 Olympics. After the U.S. boycotted those Games, Flo decided to stick around until 1984.

Flo was 6' 5" and she could spike the ball at nearly 100 miles per hour. Many people considered her the best volleyball player in the world. In 1984, the U.S. lost in the final to China and earned the silver medal.

After the Olympics, Flo played for professional teams in Italy and Japan. While sitting on the bench during a game, Flo collapsed and died. She was 31 years old. Flo was born with a disease called Marfan syndrome, which weakened her heart and caused an artery in her heart to burst.

Flo's contribution to volleyball has not been forgotten. Today, her statue stands at the U.S. Olympic Training Center in Colorado, Springs, Colorado, and the Flo Hyman Award is given annually by the Women's Sports Foundation to the athlete who captures Flo's "dignity, spirit, and commitment to excellence."

Teee Williams supplies "air" power to the U.S. attack.

FAST FACTS

- Volleyball was first called Mintonette. The name was changed in 1896 after a spectator said players seemed to be "volleying" the ball over the net.
- Volleyball became popular in Europe after U.S. soldiers played the game while stationed there during World Wars I and II.
- More than 46 million Americans play volleyball, and more than 800 million people play worldwide. Volleyball is second only to soccer in popularity.
- In 1992, the players on the U.S. men's team shaved their heads to protest a referee's decision during a match. The team's new nickname: The U.S. Volleybald Team.

hitting the ball into the air with an underhand "bump." The player holds his arms together and hits the ball with his wrists or forearms.

The second player "sets" the ball by hitting it into the air with the fingertips of both hands. The setter is a team's quarterback. He calls plays and decides who is going to spike the ball.

The hitters are usually a team's tallest and most powerful players. Their job is to spike the ball over the net.

On the other side of the net, players rush into position to set up a return. The first line of defense are the blockers. These are the same tall, powerful players who spike the ball when their team is on offense.

Two or three blockers jump and try to block the spike with their arms, or at least to slow down the ball. The blockers' teammates then hit the ball to the setter. Players dive and roll on the ground to "dig" the ball before it bounces off the floor. The team now changes from defense to offense. The setter "sets" the ball for the hitter, and the hitter spikes it over the net.

In Atlanta, 12 men's teams and 12 women's teams will compete. Italy, Brazil, and the Netherlands are the world's top men's teams. Brazil, China, and Cuba are favored in the women's tournament. The U.S. women are also strong and could sneak onto the medals stand.

STARS TO WATCH

☆ **TEEE WILLIAMS** jumps so high that she seems to have springs in her legs. In Germany, where she played professional volleyball during the 1993–94 season, she was known as the *Sprungwunder*. That means "jumping wonder" in German.

As an outside hitter, Teee, 28, plays in front of the net near the sideline. With her mix of height (5' 11") and jumping ability, Teee is a great blocker, and she hits spectacular kills. A kill is a spike that scores a point or gives the team a sideout.

The U.S. women have never won the gold medal in volleyball. Teee is thrilled that the Olympics are in Atlanta. "It will be great to be on the home court," says Teee.

Beach Volleyball

Back in the 1960's, beach volleyball was played mostly by Southern California "beach bums." Losers bought a case of beer or a steak dinner for the winners! No prize money. No television. And definitely no Olympics.

The beach game has certainly come a long way. Today, all the major tournaments are on television, and as many as 50,000 people show up at the beach to watch live action. In 1995, Karch Kiraly (see Stars to Watch) became the first player to win $2 million in his career on the beach. And in 1996, beach volleyball joins the Olympics.

Playing volleyball at the beach all day sounds like a blast. It's also a ton of work. The court size, net height, and basic rules are the same for both indoor volleyball and the beach game. But there is one important difference: Indoor teams have six players to a side. Beach teams play with two.

Having only two players to cover a full-sized court makes the game extremely difficult. Indoor players can specialize in a certain skill, such as passing, setting, or spiking. But the beach players are great all-arounders. They must be able to spike and block at the net as well as dive into the sand to dig a spike off the beach.

Men (24 teams) and women (16 teams) play a double elimination tournament. In the early rounds, the first team to score 15 points wins the game, called a set. Teams play a one-set match. In the gold medal match, sets are played to 12 points, and a team must win two-out-of-three sets to win the match.

Teams may score only while serving. Teams switch sides of the court after every five points to be fair about sun and wind conditions.

Karch Kiraly and Kent Steffes of the U.S. have been the best team in the world for the past three years. Also strong are Jan Kvalheim and Bjorn Maaseide of Norway and Ze Marco and Emanuel from Brazil.

Among the women, Sandra Pires and Jacki Silva of Brazil should challenge U.S. teams. The top U.S. players are Nancy Reno, Karolyn Kirby, Holly McPeak, and Angela Rock.

— *by Tess Reisgies*

Karch Kiraly has won two Olympic gold medals. He hopes to add a third in 1996.

STARS TO WATCH

KARCH KIRALY has already won Olympic gold medals in 1984 and 1988 with the U.S. indoor volleyball team. At the 1996 Olympics, he may win a third gold medal — this time in beach volleyball.

Karch began playing volleyball as a 6-year-old in Santa Barbara, California. His father had once played for the Hungarian junior national indoor team.

Karch played indoor volleyball in high school. He later led the University of California at Los Angeles (UCLA) to three national championships before joining the U.S. team in 1982.

Karch is considered the greatest volleyball player in the world — indoors or on the beach. He has been the top-ranked beach player since 1992. He has won more than 110 tournaments, most of them with partner Kent Steffes. Karch also has earned more than $2 million for slamming spikes in the sand.

Yachting

Ahoy! This summer, more than 400 sailors from 80 countries will compete for medals in 10 events: three men's, three women's, and four open events in which women and men may compete.

All boats in any one race are of the same design. Eight classes (or designs) of yachts will compete in the Olympics:

◆ **Europe:** These 11-footers are sailed by one woman.

◆ **Finn:** About 15 feet long, these boats are sailed by one man. Their big sails make them one of the most challenging boats to control.

◆ **470:** Pairs of men and of women compete in separate classes in these 15-foot 5-inch-long boats. The 470's are among the fastest boats in the Games.

◆ **Mistral:** These sailboards are basically surfboards with sails. The man or woman stands up on the board and holds the sail in place.

◆ **Laser:** A new Olympic class, these boats are fast, light (130 pounds), and easy to control. They are sailed by one man or woman.

◆ **Soling:** These are the longest (26' 11") and heaviest (2,281 pounds) boats. Each has a crew of three. They are sailed by men and women.

◆ **Star:** These two-person (men or women) boats are nicknamed "torture racks." They are narrow, carry huge sails, and are hard to control.

◆ **Tornado:** These are the fastest boats in the Olympics. They can hit 30 miles per hour. They are sailed by two people (men and women).

One race is held each day in each class. Boats sail a course marked by buoys and must change direction several times. The faster boats sail longer courses. An average course is 11 miles long.

The U.S. has won more Olympic yachting medals (48) than any other country. But sailors from England, Spain, New Zealand, and Australia are strong.

— *by John Rolfe*

Star-class boats are so hard to sail, they're called "torture racks."

Stars to Watch

★ **MARK REYNOLDS** and **HAL HAENEL** of the U.S. have been stars of the Star class ever since they began sailing together in 1986. They won a silver medal at the Olympics in 1988 and a gold in 1992. They are the first U.S. sailors ever to compete in two Olympics, and are going for three in 1996.

Mark, age 40, is the skipper. He was born in San Diego, California. His dad, Jim, was a Star-class world champion in 1971. Mark runs his own sailmaking business.

Hal, 37, is a former soccer player who weighs 245 pounds. His size and strength make him an ideal crew because the Star is a tough boat to handle. He is called "Hollywood Hal" because he manages a movie and TV studio in Hollywood, California.

These two will be looking for gold, not Oscars, this summer.

Weightlifting

How much do you weigh? Do you think you can lift two to three times that many pounds over your head? If you can lift that much weight, you might become an Olympic weightlifter someday.

The lifters who will compete in Atlanta are the strongest men in the world. Some can lift nearly three times their body weight. For example, Naim Suleymanoglu of Turkey *(see Stars to Watch, page 77)* weighs only 141 pounds, but he has lifted more than 420 pounds over his head.

Olympic weightlifters compete in 10 weight classes, which range from 54 kilograms (119 pounds) to more than 108 kilograms (238 pounds and over). They make two types of lifts: the snatch and the clean and jerk.

The snatch is the more difficult lift. The weight has to be lifted from the floor and over the athlete's head in one motion. It requires quickness, balance, and strength. The lifter grabs the bar between the weights and pulls up. Then quickly, he squats under the bar. While holding the bar over his head with his arms straight, he stands up.

The clean and jerk is done in two parts. First, the lifter "cleans" the weight by bending down, grabbing the bar, and lifting it to his chest. Then he "jerks" the weight by pushing it straight up as he almost jumps into a split position, with one foot in front and the other in back. The front knee is bent. He then brings his feet together and stands straight up, with the weight still up over his head.

Lifters are watched closely by three judges, who make sure a lift is done properly and the weight is under control. After the judges signal that a proper lift has been made, the lifter drops the weight to the mat.

A lifter makes three tries at each type of lift. The athlete who lifts the most total weight in the two lifts wins the gold medal in his weight class.

Weightlifting looks like a simple sport, but strategy is very important. Lifters must decide how much weight they want to put on the bar. Some lifters start by putting on a lot of weight to intimidate their opponents. Being that bold can be risky because weight may not be taken off the bar. If the lift fails, the lifter must try

Legend

Imagine you are the best weightlifter in the world. You've won two Olympic gold medals and no one has beaten you in 15 years. You'd be pretty famous, right?

Well, have you ever heard of **JOHN DAVIS**? John was an American who won his first world championship in 1938. He went on to win Olympic gold medals in the super-heavyweight division in 1948 and 1952. Few Americans heard of John until 1953, when he *lost* for the first time in 15 years!

Weightlifting was much more popular in Europe than in the U.S. while John was competing. In Europe, John was a superstar. The citizens of France admired him so much he was offered a house there and a good deal of money.

JOHN DAVIS

John died in 1984. His lack of fame in America once made him say, "I was born in the wrong country at the wrong time." Which is too bad. If he were alive and competing today, the U.S. weightlifting team could really use him in Atlanta!

Fast Facts

- Weightlifting is one of the world's oldest sports. In ancient times, people competed by lifting large stones.
- Weightlifting became a modern Olympic sport in 1896. There was only one weight class (super-heavyweight) and athletes competed in one-hand lift and two-hand lift. The modern snatch and clean and jerk lifts have been used since 1928.
- Weight classes in international competition were changed in 1993. All Olympic records that were set before this year no longer count. The best lifts in Atlanta will all be records.
- The world record for the most weight raised in one Olympic-style lift is a 587-pound clean and jerk, set by Leonid Taranenko of the Soviet Union in 1988.

again. If he succeeds, he gets to choose how much weight to add for his next lift. A minimum of 2.5 kilograms (6.25 pounds) must be added.

The competition in Atlanta should be very exciting. Two lifters, Turkey's Naim Suleymanoglu and Alexander Kurlovich of Belarus, could make history. Both have won two Olympic gold medals. They will try to become the first lifters to win three golds. Manfred Nerlinger of Germany will try to become the second lifter ever to win four Olympic medals.

The top teams are from Russia, Turkey, and China, which won the team competition at the 1995 world championships. Germany, Greece, Bulgaria, and Belarus have strong teams, too.

Alexander Kurlovich of Belarus hopes to win a historic third gold medal in Atlanta.

Unfortunately, lifters from the U.S. will have a hard time winning medals in Atlanta. The U.S. team did very poorly at last year's world championships. The top eight teams at that event can send 10 lifters to the Olympics. The U.S. finished 31st and may not be allowed to send more than three lifters. Super-heavyweight Mark Henry finished a disappointing 15th at the worlds. It now seems unlikely that he will win a medal in Atlanta.

The U.S. team's performance was disappointing, but rooting for underdogs can be fun.

— *by John Rolfe*

Stars to Watch

NAIM SULEYMANOGLU of Turkey is only 5 feet tall and weighs 141 pounds, but he is so strong, he is nicknamed "Pocket Hercules."

Naim may be the greatest weightlifter of all time. He has won two Olympic gold medals and nine world championships, and he holds all three world records in his weight class.

Naim is Turkish, but he grew up in the Eastern European country of Bulgaria. By age 15, Naim had become the youngest weightlifter ever to set a world record. At 16, he was only the second man ever to lift three times his own body weight.

In Bulgaria, the government began mistreating Turks. Naim was so angry that he sneaked away from his team at a 1986 tournament in Australia. He is now a citizen of Turkey.

Naim won his gold medals at the 1988 and 1992 Games. This year, he wants to become the first lifter ever to win three. Naim should be up to the task.

Wrestling

Olympic wrestling is not Wrestlemania. You won't see wild-eyed guys in kooky costumes stomping each other. You *will* see intense action where quickness, strength, and control are keys.

There are two types of Olympic wrestling: freestyle and Greco-Roman. In freestyle, a wrestler may grab his opponent's legs, and he may use his own legs to hold or pin an opponent. In Greco-Roman, a wrestler may not use his legs to hold an opponent, or grab an opponent below the hips.

Wrestlers compete in 10 weight classes, ranging from light-flyweight (99 to 105.5 pounds) to super-heavyweight (220 to 286 pounds). A match consists of one five-minute period. A wrestler wins by getting a "pin" (holding an opponent's shoulder blades to the mat for half a second), by scoring the most points, or by building up a 10-point lead.

Points are scored in several ways. Throwing an opponent from a standing position onto his back is worth 5 points. If the opponent gets off his back, he gets 1 point for an "escape." Other moves are worth 2 or 3 points. The closer a move puts an opponent in danger of being pinned, the more it is worth.

If the score is tied, or if neither wrestler has scored 3 points after five minutes, a three-minute overtime period is held.

Freestyle

Freestyle wrestling is similar to high school and college wrestling. Matches begin with both wrestlers on their feet. At the referee's signal, the wrestlers attack and try to take their opponent to the mat. A freestyle wrestler often tries to get a takedown by grabbing one or both of his opponent's legs.

The U.S. has won more Olympic freestyle medals (94) than any other country. The U.S. should add to its medal count in Atlanta. It could have eight current or past world champions on the 1996 team, including super-heavyweight Bruce Baumgartner *(see Stars to Watch, page 79)* and Kurt Angle in the heavyweight (220 pounds) class.

Kevin Jackson won the gold medal in the middleweight division (180.5 pounds) at the 1992 Olympics. In 1995, he came back from shoulder and neck injuries to win the world championship. Kevin is a master at stopping opponents' moves

FREESTYLE Double-Leg Takedown

GRECO-ROMAN Headlock Throw

TAKEDOWNS

In both freestyle and Greco-Roman, a wrestler's first objective at the beginning of a match is to to throw the other wrestler to the mat. This is called a takedown and is worth 1 point. In freestyle, wrestlers may attack an opponent's legs. The double-leg takedown is a common freestyle move. In Greco-Roman, wrestlers are not allowed to grab an opponent below his hips. The headlock throw is a popular Greco-Roman takedown.

Kevin Jackson of the U.S. *(in blue)* crushed Elmadi Jabrailov of the Unified Team for the 1992 gold.

and quickly counterattacking.

Other medal contenders for the U.S. include 1995 bantamweight (125.5 pounds) world champion Terry Brands and his twin brother, Tom. Tom competes in the featherweight (136.5 pounds) class.

The U.S. should be challenged by a strong Russian team. Russia finished third at the 1995 world championships. Russia was once a part of the Soviet Union, which broke up in 1991. The Soviet team won every world freestyle championship from 1962 to 1992. Several members of the current Russian team used to compete for the Soviet Union.

Russia's best freestyler is Makharbek Khadartsev, a light-heavyweight (198.5 pounds). He won Olympic gold medals in 1988 and 1992. He will try to become the second wrestler to win gold in three straight Olympics.

Iran finished a strong second to the U.S. at the 1995 world championships. Rasul Khadem won the bronze medal as a middleweight (180.5 pounds) at the 1992 Olympics. He then moved up to light-heavyweight and beat Makharbek Khadartsev for the gold medal at the 1994 world championships.

Turkey, a country in the Middle East, is also strong. Super-heavyweight Mahmut Demir could be Bruce Baumgartner's toughest challenger. Mahmut defeated Bruce at the 1994 world championships.

STARS TO WATCH

In high school, **BRUCE BAUMGARTNER** was not a great wrestler. He was pinned in his first match. As a senior, in 1978, he finished third in the New Jersey state championships. People might have laughed if they had been told Bruce would become the greatest American freestyle wrestler of all time.

Bruce is now a three-time freestyle super-heavyweight world champion. In Atlanta, he will defend his 1992 Olympic gold medal and try to become the first freestyle wrestler to win medals in four Olympics. Bruce won gold at the 1984 Games and silver in 1988.

Off the mat, Bruce likes to work in his garden, collect stamps, and make furniture.

Greco-Roman

Scoring points in Greco-Roman wrestling takes hard work and lots of muscle. Upper-body strength is important because a wrestler must lift an opponent, then throw him to the mat to score points.

Russia has won every Greco-Roman world championship since 1992. It could have as many as five Olympic medalists competing in Atlanta. The team's captain is super-heavyweight Alexander Karelin *(see Stars to Watch)*.

Another Russian star is Sergei Martinov. Sergei won the silver medal at the 1992 Olympics in the 136.5-pound class. He also has won world championships in 1991, 1993, 1994, and 1995.

Germany also has several strong Greco-Roman wrestlers. Light-heavyweight Maik Bullman won an Olympic gold medal in 1992. Two of his teammates, light-flyweight Oleg Koutcherenko and flyweight Alfred Ter Mkrtchyan, used to compete for the Soviet Union. Both won Olympic medals in 1992.

U.S. wrestlers have won only two Olympic Greco-Roman gold medals. Both were surprises. In 1984, Steven Fraser won a gold medal in the light-heavyweight (198.5 pounds) class and Jeffrey Blatnick won the super-heavyweight gold. Jeffrey's victory was special because he had battled cancer two years before the Olympics.

The next surprise for the U.S. could be bantamweight (125.5 pounds) Dennis Hall. At the 1995 worlds, Dennis upset four former world champions in five matches to win the gold medal.

Super-heavyweight Matt Ghaffari could also be a U.S. surprise. He is the only wrestler ever to last a full five-minute match plus an overtime against Alexander Karelin. Matt was born in Iran but moved to the U.S. when he was 15.

In Atlanta, the U.S. could finish as high as second if all goes well. If not, it could finish as low as 10th.

– by John Rolfe

Russia's Alexander Karelin tries to turn Matt Ghaffari of the U.S. at the 1992 Olympics.

Fast Facts

- **The Greeks held wrestling events in the Olympics as far back as 704 B.C. (The word Greco means "Greek.") The Romans copied the Greek sport in their festivals.**
- **Milo of Croton won five Olympic titles between 536 B.C. and 520 B.C. He once ate a bull after carrying it on his shoulders around the Olympic arena.**

Stars to Watch

★ Super-heavyweight **ALEXANDER KARELIN** of Russia may be the greatest Greco-Roman wrestler of all time. He has never lost in international competition. In Atlanta, he will try to become the second wrestler to win gold medals at three straight Olympics.

Alexander is very big and strong. He once carried a refrigerator up eight flights of stairs!

Watch for Alexander's awesome move called the "reverse body lift." When an opponent is lying on his stomach, Alexander grabs him around the waist, lifts him off the mat, and flips him onto his back. *Bam!* Then he pins him.

Alexander is called "The Siberian Bear." He was born in Siberia, a cold, snowy area in northeastern Russia. He once trained by running in snow up to his thighs.

Alexander has plenty of smarts to go with his muscle. He likes to read, write poetry, and listen to classical music in his spare time.

What Do You Know?

Here's your chance to be an Olympic champion! Use your knowledge of the Summer Games to answer these questions. Then turn to page 96 to see how you did.

1. What famous pro athlete *won't* be competing in Atlanta?
a. Tennis player Monica Seles
b. Baseball player Ken Griffey, Junior
c. NBA star Reggie Miller
d. Cyclist Miguel Induráin

2. Mark Spitz won seven gold medals in 1972. It was the most gold medals ever won in a single sport at the same Olympics. In what sport did Mark win those medals?

3. In 1992, Michael Jordan played in his second Olympics. When was his first?
a. Moscow, Russia, 1980
b. Melbourne, Australia, 1956
c. Los Angeles, Calif., 1984
d. Seoul, South Korea, 1988

4. How many events make up the heptathlon?

5. IZZY is the official mascot of the 1996 Games. Who was the first official Summer Games mascot, in 1976?
a. Amik the Beaver
b. Misha the Bear
c. Tony the Tiger
d. Cobi the Dog

6. Of the following athletes, who did *not* wear shoes when he won a gold medal?
a. Carl Lewis (the 100-meter sprint, in 1984)
b. Abebe Bikila (marathon, 1960)
c. Forrest Gump (javelin, 1980)
d. Al Oerter (discus, 1956)

7. True or false: Only countries that win medals are invited to the next Olympics.

8. When did women first compete at the Olympics?
a. 1924   b. 1900
c. 1988   d. 1896

9. What Olympic sport combines soccer and basketball rules and is played indoors?

10. What event has never been an Olympic sport?
a. Golf   b. Tug of War
c. Darts   d. Croquet

11. American Greg Louganis won both diving events in 1984 *and* in 1988. One event was the springboard and the other was the _____.

12. This is a picture of the first gymnast to score a perfect 10 at the Olympics. She did it in 1976. Who is she?

13. True or false: The first Olympic basketball tournament, in 1936, was played outdoors on clay courts.

14. In 1960, Cassius Clay won a gold medal in boxing. This heavyweight champion was later known as _____.

15. In Atlanta, women will compete in two team sports for the first time. What sports?

16. Worldwide, how many people are expected to watch the 1996 Olympics on TV?
a. 35,000
b. 3,500,000
c. 3,500,000,000

17. Besides Atlanta, two U.S cities have hosted the Summer Games. Which city has *not* hosted the Olympics?
a. St. Louis, Missouri
b. Los Angeles, California
c. New York, New York

Welcome to Atlanta

Atlanta will be the center of action during the 1996 Games. Most events will take place at stadiums and arenas near Atlanta or inside the "Olympic ring," an imaginary circle in central Atlanta. Several sports will be held elsewhere in Georgia, and a few will be in other states. Here are the sports locations, and some points of interest, in Atlanta.

1. **Alexander Memorial Coliseum** Boxing
2. **Georgia Tech Aquatic Center** Swimming, Diving, Synchronized Swimming, Water Polo, Modern Pentathlon
3. **Georgia World Congress Center** Fencing, Team Handball, Judo, Modern Pentathlon, Table Tennis, Weightlifting, Wrestling
4. **Omni Coliseum** Indoor Volleyball
5. **Georgia Dome** Basketball, Gymnastics, Team Handball
6. **Morris Brown College** Field Hockey
7. **Clark Atlanta University** Field Hockey
8. **Morehouse College** Basketball
9. **Atlanta-Fulton County Stadium** Baseball
10. **Olympic Stadium** Opening and closing ceremonies, Track and Field
11. **Georgia State University** Badminton
12. **Zoo Atlanta** One of the country's best zoos, in Grant Park. Nearby are Fort Walker and the Cyclorama (a Civil War museum).
13. **Martin Luther King, Jr. National Historic Site** The great civil rights leader lived here. Visitors can see his birthplace (now a museum), his church, and his grave.
14. **Stone Mountain Park** Archery, Cycling, Tennis
15. **Georgia International Horse Park** Equestrian, Modern Pentathlon, Mountain Biking
16. **Atlanta Beach** Beach Volleyball
17. **Wolf Creek Shooting Complex** Shooting, Modern Pentathlon

The Olympic Ring

DID YOU KNOW?

- Atlanta is Georgia's largest city and its capital. It was first called "Terminus," because it was the end of a railroad line.
- During the Civil War, Union General William Sherman captured Atlanta and burned much of it down.
- Atlanta's symbol is the phoenix, a mythological bird that rose from its own ashes.
- Stone Mountain is the largest mass of exposed granite in the world. It has a huge (90' x 190') carving of General Robert E. Lee and two other famous Confederates.
- In 1974, Hank Aaron of the Atlanta Braves hit his 715th career home run, at Atlanta-Fulton County Stadium, to break Babe Ruth's record.
- Atlanta has 55 streets with the words *peach tree* in their names.

Moments to Remember

JESSE OWENS AND LUZ LONG, 1936

Jesse Owens won four gold medals at the Berlin Olympics, in 1936. One of those medals was in the long jump, and he might never have won it if it weren't for the good sportsmanship of Germany's Luz Long.

In the qualifying round, Jesse kept stepping over the foul line, which meant his jumps didn't count. He had one last jump to qualify. He was scared that he would step over the line again. Then, Luz came over to help. Luz could have won the gold medal if Jesse were not in the finals, but he *wanted* Jesse to compete. This angered Germany's leader, Adolf Hitler. Hitler believed that white athletes were better than black athletes.

Luz didn't agree with Hitler. He told Jesse to put a towel a foot in front of the foul line and to take off *in front* of the towel.

Jesse took Luz's advice and easily qualified for the finals. Then he defeated seven jumpers, including Luz, to win the gold medal. Luz was the first person to congratulate Jesse after he won. In the spirit of Olympic friendship, they walked a victory lap together.

Luz *(left)* **gave Jesse some friendly advice in the long jump.**

LIS HARTEL, 1952

In 1944, Lis Hartel of Denmark contracted polio, a disease that left her

Lis had to be helped into her saddle but she still won a silver medal!

unable to walk without crutches. Lis had been an excellent dressage [*dreh-SAHJ*] rider before her illness. She was determined to compete again

At the 1952 Olympics, in Helsinki, Finland, Lis was one of four women who qualified to compete against men in dressage. Lis was still paralyzed below the knees. She had to be helped on and off her horse.

While she was on, though, Lis was amazing. Lis guided her horse through the course beautifully and won the silver medal! At the victory ceremony, the crowd cheered wildly as Lis was helped onto the medal podium by gold medal winner Henry St. Cyr of Sweden.

1896   ATHENS, GREECE
Countries: 13   Athletes: 311
- The first Olympic Games in 1,500 years take place in Greece, site of the ancient Olympics from 776 B.C. to A.D. 394. All of the competitors at the 1896 Olympic Games are male.

1900   PARIS, FRANCE
Countries: 22   Athletes: 1,330
- Women compete in the Olympics for the first time. Margaret Abbott of the United States and Charlotte Cooper of Great Britain are the first female gold medal winners. Margaret wins the women's nine-hole golf tournament. Charlotte wins the women's singles title in tennis.

1904   ST. LOUIS, MISSOURI
Countries: 12   Athletes: 687
- Many European athletes do not attend the Games because the U.S. is too far away from Europe. As a result, Americans win 238 of the 284 medals.
- American George Poage becomes the first black man to compete in the Olympics. He places third in the hurdles.

Four years later, Lis won another silver medal in dressage at the 1956 Games.

PAAVO NURMI, 1924

At the 1924 Games, in Paris, France, Paavo Nurmi of Finland lived up to his nickname, the Flying Finn, and proved that he was the greatest runner alive. Over four days, Paavo won *five* track-and-field gold medals.

Paavo's first gold came in the 1,500-meter race. Carrying a stopwatch in his hand, he ran as fast as a sprinter would for the first 400 meters and then "coasted" to an Olympic record.

Within an hour, Paavo was back on the track for the 5,000 meters. The rest of the runners knew Paavo would be tired, so they tried to run at a fast pace to wear him down. But he managed to stay close to the pack and then pulled ahead at the halfway mark. He won by two yards, setting another Olympic record and amazing everyone. Paavo had run two great races and won two gold medals in 1½ hours!

Two days later, Paavo won the 10,000-meter cross-country race in unbearable heat. The weather and course were so

Paavo won five long-distance-running medals at the 1924 Games.

bad that 23 of the 38 runners who started the race never finished! He earned gold medals for individual and team victories in the race.

The next day, Paavo won his fifth gold medal, in the 3,000-meter team race.

PAT MCCORMICK, 1956

Pat McCormick climbed the platform for her final dive at the Melbourne Games. Pat had won gold medals in springboard *and* platform diving at the 1952 Olympics. And she had already repeated her victory in the 1956 springboard event.

Now she wanted to win the platform medal, but she was in third place with two dives to go. Pat did a tricky dive and she did it beautifully! She went on to the gold and became the first athlete ever to win gold medals in both diving events!

JOHN AKHWARI, 1968

Marathon runner John Stephen Akhwari of Tanzania didn't win any medals at the Mexico City Olympics, but he showed plenty of Olympic spirit.

More than an hour after Mamo Wolde of Ethiopia had won the race, John staggered into the Olympic stadium. His right leg was bandaged and bloody from a fall. Still, John hobbled slowly on.

Only a few thousand fans remained in the stands. They all cheered for John as if he were the winner. Finally, John crossed the finish line, the last runner to complete the race.

Later, John was asked why he didn't drop out after his injury. "My country did not send me to Mexico City to start the race," John answered. "They sent me to finish the race."

— *by Bob Der*

1908 LONDON, ENGLAND
Countries: 23   Athletes: 2,035
- Figure skating makes its first Olympic appearance . . . as a summer sport!

1912 STOCKHOLM, SWEDEN
Countries: 28   Athletes: 2,547
- Women's swimming is held in the Olympics for the first time. Australia's Fanny Durack wins the only event, the 100-meter freestyle.

1916
- The Olympic Games are cancelled because of World War I.

1920 ANTWERP, BELGIUM
Countries: 29   Athletes: 2,517
- The Olympic symbol of five interlocking rings appears for the first time. The rings symbolize brotherhood among countries.

Simply Amazing

Olympic history is full of amazing stories. Here are a few.

BAREFOOT IN THE PARK . . .

and on the street . . . and around the track . . . Runner Abebe Bikila of Ethiopia won the men's marathon in Rome, in 1960, and again at the Tokyo Games, in 1964. He was the first person to win two Olympic marathons.

But that isn't Abebe's only claim to fame: During the 1960 marathon, he ran the entire course — all 26 miles and 385 yards — wearing *no shoes!*

Abebe wore no shoes!

ONCE MORE FOR FUN

After four hours of hard cycling in 93-degree heat, Viktor Kapitonov couldn't wait for the 108-mile road race at the 1960 Olympics to end. The Soviet cyclist sprinted and crossed the finish line first, just ahead of Livio Trapé of Italy.

But the race wasn't over! Viktor had another nine-mile lap to go. About 24 minutes later, Viktor sprinted across the finish line again, just inches ahead of Livio. This time he *did* win the gold!

FOREVER YOUNG

Ulrike Meyfarth of West Germany was 16 years old when she competed in the women's high jump at the 1972 Olympics. But she wasn't exactly a little girl: She was 6 feet tall! And she jumped 6' 3½" to tie the world record and win the gold medal. The performance made this big-little girl the *youngest* individual winner in Olympic track-and-field history.

Twelve years later, at the Los Angeles Games, Ulrike set an Olympic record and won the women's high jump again. She also set another age record: She became the *oldest* person to win the Olympic high jump.

Ulrike set two age records.

LET'S DIS-CUS THIS

A 20-year-old college student named Al Oerter won the discus competition at the 1956 Games, in Melbourne. He set an Olympic record of 184' 11". No one else's throw was close!

1924   PARIS, FRANCE
Countries: 44   Athletes: 3,092
- America's Johnny Weissmuller wins three gold medals in freestyle swimming and a bronze medal in water polo. Johnny went on to play Tarzan in 18 movies!

1928   AMSTERDAM, THE NETHERLANDS
Countries: 46   Athletes: 3,014
- The Olympic flame makes its first appearance. The flame burns throughout the Games.
- Women compete in gymnastics and track and field for the first time.

1932   LOS ANGELES, CALIFORNIA
Countries: 37   Athletes: 1,408
- The first Olympic Village is built for athletes to live in during the Games. It is for men only.
- Babe Didrikson of the U.S. enters, and wins, three women's track and field events. She wanted to enter more but wasn't allowed to.

In 1960, Al competed at Rome and won another gold with *another* Olympic-record throw (194' 2"). In 1964, Al tore cartilage in his ribs less than a week before the Olympic discus competition, but he still won — with *another* Olympic record (200' 1").

In 1968, Al entered the discus again. He was 32 years old. After two rounds of the finals, he was in fourth place. Then he let loose with a toss of 212' 6", five feet further than he had ever thrown the discus in his life! He won the gold medal again and became the first, and only, athlete to win the same event in four Olympics in a row.

Al won four discus titles!

OUT-STAND-ING!

Here's an Olympian feat that no one will ever top: From 1900 through 1908, Raymond Ewry of the U.S. won eight gold medals: three each in the standing high jump and standing long jump, and two in the standing triple jump. (That event wasn't held in 1908, or he might have won it, too.)

No one else has ever won as many jumping gold medals as that and no one ever will — at least in Ray's events. Standing jumps have not been included in the Olympics since 1912.

UNBEATABLE DAWN

At the 1956 Games, in Melbourne, Australia swimmer Dawn Fraser won three medals, including a gold in the women's 100-meter freestyle.

The world record for the 100 had been broken *six* times by three swimmers that year. Dawn broke the record again when she won the gold — and held it for the next 15 years!

Dawn went on to win the 100 meters at the 1960 *and* the 1964 Games. That made her the first swimmer — male or female — to win the same individual event three times!

— *by Marie MacNee*

Events You Won't See

Believe it or not, these once were Olympic events:
- **Tug-of-war** was a part of the Olympics from 1900 through 1920. Two teams of men tried to pull each other six feet. If neither could do it in five minutes, the team that had pulled the farthest won.
- At the Paris Games, in 1900, **croquet** [*crow-KAY*] was on the schedule. French men swept the medals in all three events — singles, one ball; singles, two ball; and doubles.
- In the early days of the Olympics, there were some unusual **swimming** events: the obstacle race (1900), underwater swimming (1900), and the plunge for distance (1904). There's always a chance they could reappear . . . but don't hold your breath.

1936 BERLIN, GERMANY
Countries: 49   Athletes: 4,066
- The Torch Relay is run for the first time. The torch holds the Olympic flame and is carried through seven countries by 3,000 runners.
- Jesse Owens (right) of the U.S. wins four track-and-field gold medals.
- Basketball becomes an Olympic sport.

1940, 1944
- The Olympic Games are cancelled twice because of World War II.

1948 LONDON, ENGLAND,
Countries: 59   Athletes: 4,099
- America's Alice Coachman wins the women's high jump. Alice is the first black woman to win an Olympic gold medal.
- Fanny Blankers-Koen of the Netherlands sets a women's Olympic record by winning four gold medals in track and field. Her record still stands.

Whatizit? and Other Questions

Izzy, the 1996 mascot

Have Olympic athletes always won medals?

Today, every athlete who wins an Olympic event gets a gold medal. Second-place finishers receive a silver medal, and those who come in third earn a bronze. *Everyone* who competes in the Olympics gets a simple medal and a diploma for participating. But that wasn't always the case.

At the ancient Olympic Games, winners received a wreath of wild-olive leaves that came from a sacred grove in Olympia. No one else got anything.

Since 1928, Olympic medals have all had the same images: a woman holding palm leaves and an olive wreath; a stadium; a horse-drawn chariot; a Grecian urn; and the five rings.

Whatizit?

That's what many people asked when Izzy, the mascot of the 1996 games, was officially introduced in 1992. In fact, that was Izzy's original name ("Whatizit"). Izzy is a computer-generated blue blob with lightning bolts for eyebrows. The mascot can change into many Olympic forms. For example, add some boxing gloves and padded headgear, and Izzy turns into Itzaboxer! You will probably see Izzy a lot during the Games.

Sam the Eagle

Mascots are a familiar sight at many sports events. They are symbols of good luck. At the Olympics, they first appeared in 1968. Here are some of them:

♦ The first official Olympic mascot was Amik the Beaver. He was the mascot of the

1952 HELSINKI, FINLAND
Countries: 69 **Athletes:** 4,925
● Athletes from the Soviet Union compete in the Olympics for the first time, winning 71 medals.

1956 MELBOURNE, AUSTRALIA
Countries: 67 **Athletes:** 3,342
● The Games run from November 22 to December 8 because Australia is in the Southern Hemisphere, where seasons are the opposite of those in the Northern Hemisphere.
● America's Al Oerter wins a gold medal in the discus. Al goes on to win the event in the next three Olympics!

1960 ROME, ITALY
Countries: 83 **Athletes:** 5,348
● Cassius Clay of the U.S. wins a gold medal in light-heavyweight boxing. Cassius later becomes heavyweight champion of the world and changes his name to Muhammad Ali.
● The Games are televised in the U.S. by CBS.

1976 Summer Games, held in Montreal, Quebec, Canada.

◆ Misha, a cuddly brown bear, was the mascot at the only Olympics hosted by the Soviet Union — the 1980 Moscow Summer Games.

◆ Sam the Eagle, of the 1984 Olympics, in Los Angeles, California, was the first U.S. Summer Games mascot.

When was the Olympic torch relay first run?

The Olympic flame became a part of the modern Games in 1928, at Amsterdam. The first relay was held before the 1936 Games. Some 3,000 runners carried torches from the Temple of Zeus, in Olympia, Greece, to Berlin, Germany.

The Olympic torch

The Olympic flag

Why does the Olympic flag have five rings?

The five interlocking rings were inspired by a design on an altar at the ancient Greek city of Delphi. There is no official meaning to them. Many people believe that the five colors (blue, yellow, black, green, and red) stand for the continents: Africa, the Americas, Asia, Europe, and Oceania. Supposedly, at least one of these five colors can be found in the flag of every nation. In any case, the Olympic rings have become a symbol of international brotherhood.

The rings made their first appearance in 1914. That was the 20th anniversary of the founding of the International Olympic Committee (IOC). To celebrate the occasion, Baron Pierre de Coubertin, the father of the modern Games, gave the Olympic Congress a flag. In the center of this plain white flag were the rings. The flag flew in Olympia, Greece, that year and, six years later, flew at the Antwerp Games. (The 1916 Olympics were canceled because of World War I.)

The Olympic flag is passed from one Olympics to the next. At the closing ceremonies, the mayor of the host city presents it to the mayor of the next host city. It is kept in the town hall of the new host city until the next Olympics.

— *by Marie MacNee*

1964 TOKYO, JAPAN
Countries: 93 Athletes: 5,140
- Tokyo becomes the first Asian country ever to host the Olympics.
- America's Bob Hayes wins gold medals in the 100-meter dash and the 4x100-meter relay. After the Olympics, Bob plays pro football with the Dallas Cowboys, as a wide receiver.

1968 MEXICO CITY, MEXICO
Countries: 112 Athletes: 5,531
- Dick Fosbury of the U.S. wins the high jump with a new jumping technique that he invented: the "Fosbury Flop."

1972 MUNICH, WEST GERMANY
Countries: 122 Athletes: 7,147
- Gymnast Olga Korbut of the Soviet Union becomes the first female gymnast to do a backflip on the balance beam. She wins a gold medal in that event, and another gold in the floor exercise.

The World of the

In 100 years of modern Olympics, cities all over the world have hosted the Summer Games

Many countries have won medals at the Summer Games. Here are the top 20.

COUNTRY	GOLD	SILVER	BRONZE
United States	781	604	522
Soviet Union/Russia	418	297	296
Great Britain	169	215	215
France	137	146	172
Germany (EAST & WEST)	132	152	140
Hungary	133	120	141
Sweden	113	125	140
Italy	147	108	119
Finland	101	77	111
Australia	73	68	88
Romania	59	64	90
Poland	43	59	101
Canada	44	66	82
Bulgaria	40	69	57
The Netherlands	45	52	69
Switzerland	37	60	56
Denmark	32	57	56
Czechoslovakia	46	48	43
China	36	41	37
Belgium	33	40	39

1904 St Louis, Missouri

1976 Montreal, Canada

1932, 1984 Los Angeles, California

1996 Atlanta, Georgia

1968 Mexico City, Mexico

1976 MONTREAL, CANADA
Countries: 92   Athletes: 6,085
- America's Sugar Ray Leonard wins the light-welterweight boxing title. He goes on to become a wildly popular and successful pro boxer.

1980 MOSCOW, SOVIET UNION
Countries: 81   Athletes: 5,353
- Many countries, including the U.S., choose not to compete because the Soviet Union (the host country) had invaded Afghanistan the year before.
- Soviet gymnast Aleksandr Ditiatin wins eight medals, the most ever by an athlete in a single Olympics. He also becomes the first male gymnast to score a perfect 10 in the Olympics.

1984 LOS ANGELES, CALIFORNIA
Countries: 141   Athletes: 7,078
- Greg Louganis of the U.S. wins gold medals in both platform and springboard diving. Greg is the first male to win both events since 1928.

Summer Games

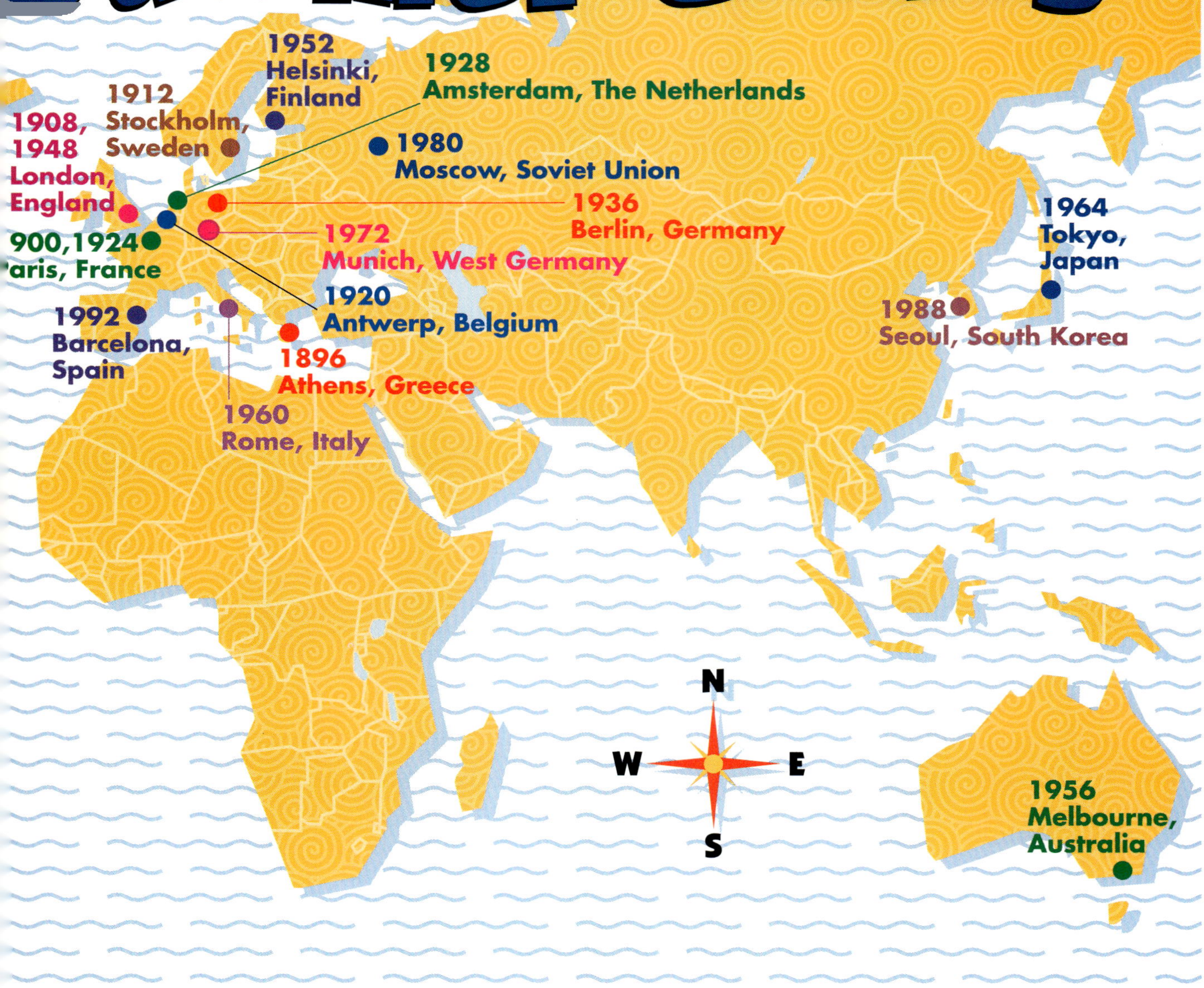

- 1952 Helsinki, Finland
- 1928 Amsterdam, The Netherlands
- 1912 Stockholm, Sweden
- 1908, 1948 London, England
- 1980 Moscow, Soviet Union
- 1936 Berlin, Germany
- 1964 Tokyo, Japan
- 1900, 1924 Paris, France
- 1972 Munich, West Germany
- 1992 Barcelona, Spain
- 1920 Antwerp, Belgium
- 1988 Seoul, South Korea
- 1896 Athens, Greece
- 1960 Rome, Italy
- 1956 Melbourne, Australia

1988 SEOUL, SOUTH KOREA
Countries: 159 Athletes: 9,421
- America's Jackie Joyner-Kersee earns the title of the world's greatest female athlete by winning gold medals in the heptathlon and the long jump.
- Tennis returns to the Olympics as a medal sport for the first time in 64 years. Germany's Steffi Graf wins the women's singles.

1992 BARCELONA, SPAIN
Countries: 172 Athletes: 10,563
- America's Dream Team, the greatest basketball team ever, runs away with the gold. Led by Michael Jordan and Patrick Ewing (right), the Dream Team wins its games by an average of 43.8 points!

1996 ATLANTA, GEORGIA
Countries: 197
Athletes (estimated): 10,700
- The modern Olympic Games gets ready to celebrate its 100th birthday!

Guess Who?

Each set of pictures and letters below represents the name of an Olympic "Star to Watch." Add or subtract to sound out the names. (To help, we've given you the athlete's sport.) Print the names below each set, and then copy the letters in the blue boxes onto the "Letters" line. Unscramble *those* letters to see what these stars hope to be by the end of the Games.

SOFTBALL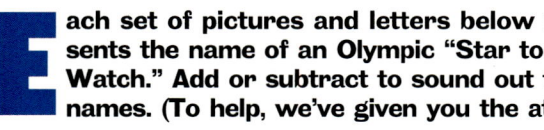

VOLLEYBALL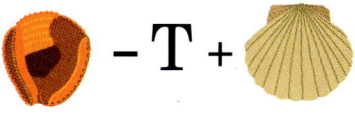

TRACK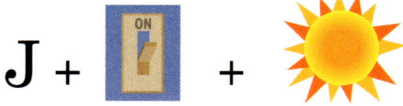

CYCLING

THE LETTERS: ___ ___ ___ ___ ___ ___ ___

THE ANSWER: ___ ___ ___ ___ ___ ___ ___

The SUM-mer Games

| 2 | 10 | 5 |
| 4 | 11 | 7 |

Athletes from 197 nations will be competing at the 1996 Olympics. Use the numbers in the yellow box above to fill in the blanks. (Each number may be used only once.) Then do the arithmetic indicated, using the numbers you've filled in. The total will tell you how many countries participated in the first modern Olympics, in 1896.
 Check your answer on page 96.

The number of rings on the Olympic flag ___
Dream Team member David Robinson is ___ feet tall **+** ___
Number of people on each side in beach volleyball **−** ___
Events in the decathlon **+** ___
Years between the Summer Olympics **+** ___
Number of soccer teammates on the field at one time **−** ___
TOTAL: **=** ___

Olympic Word Spiral

Use what you know about the Olympic Games to fill in the answers in the grid in a clockwise direction. Each correct word ends at the space in which you see the next number. The last letter of each word will be the first letter of the next word.

We've done the first one for you. The answer, WEIGHTLIFTERS, ends in an *s*, so the second word must begin with an *s*. Because there are four spaces between number 2 and number 3, the word must be a four-letter word. When you've filled in all the words, the shaded column in the center of the grid should spell out the name of an Olympic sport. The answers are on page 96.

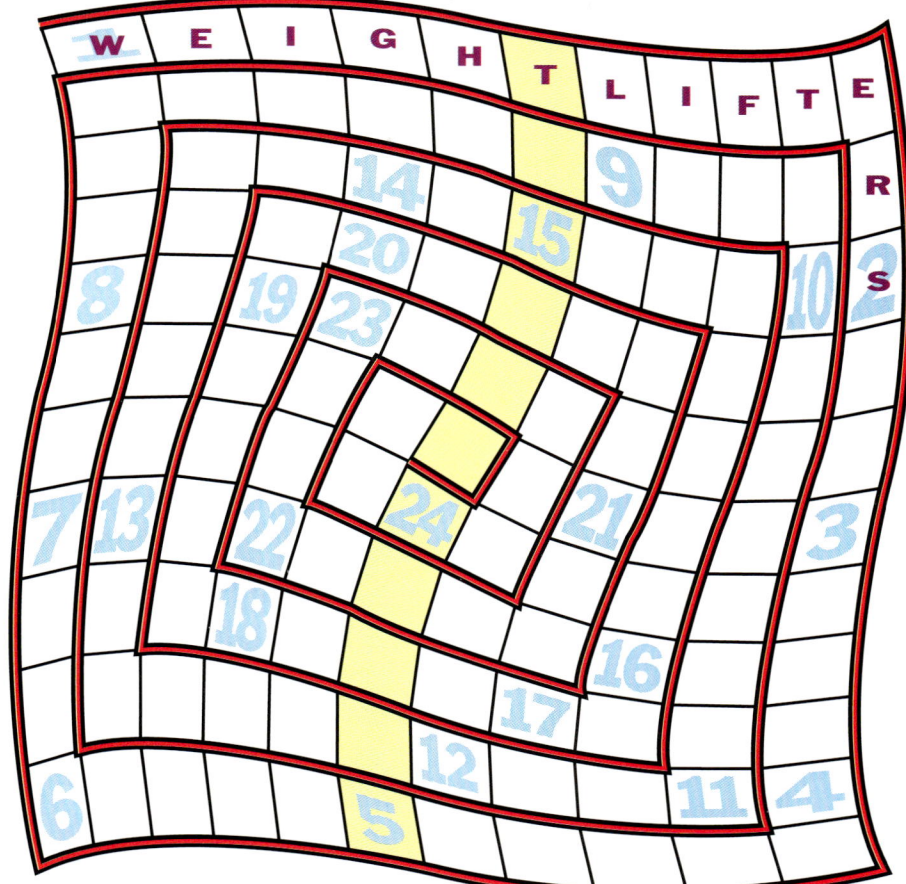

1. These athletes "snatch" barbells.
2. A track-and-field event: the _____ put
3. A _____ is used to carry the Olympic flame.
4. In certain races, runners have to jump over these.
5. Decathletes have to be fast and _____.
6. The winner of an Olympic event wins a ____ medal.
7. The l00-meter ____
8. An event for male gymnasts: the _____ bar
9. Carl ____ has won eight Olympic gold medals in track and field.
10. Backstroke, butterfly, and freestyle are different _____ strokes.
11. One of this sport's biggest tournaments (the Masters' championship) is played in the state that is hosting the 1996 Summer Olympics. This non-Olympic sport is called _____.
12. In baseball, the shortstop is usually one of the best _____.
13. One of the new official sports for women at the 1996 Olympics is _____.
14. A high, arcing shot in tennis
15. The 1992 Summer Olympics were held in _____, Spain.
16. 1992 Dream Team member: Michael "___" Jordan
17. The Olympic symbol has five colored ____.
18. Olympians who come in second get _____ medals.
19. The referee at a basketball game is called ____ for short.
20. Pro sports teams in Atlanta include baseball's Braves, basketball's Hawks, and football's _____.
21. U.S. gymnastic star _____ Miller.
22. Water-polo players score by throwing balls into ____.
23. In this track event, runners must jump over 28 hurdles and seven water jumps. It's called the _____ chase.
24. Germany used to be divided into two countries, ____ and West.

The Schedule

The action will be non-stop during the 16 days of competition at the Summer Games. Here's a complete schedule of the final game, race, bout, or performance for each of the 271 events.

JULY 20
WEIGHTLIFTING: 54 kilogram
SHOOTING: Men's 10-meter air pistol
Women's 10-meter air rifle
FENCING: Men's individual épée
JUDO: Men's heavyweight
Women's heavyweight
SWIMMING: Women's 100-meter freestyle
Men's 100-meter breaststroke
Women's 400-meter individual medley
Men's 200-meter freestyle

JULY 21
SWIMMING: Women's 200-meter freestyle
Men's 400-meter individual medley
Women's 100-meter breaststroke
Men's 4x200-meter freestyle relay
CYCLING: Women's road race
SHOOTING: Women's 10-meter air pistol
Men's trap shooting
WEIGHTLIFTING: 59 kilograms
FENCING: Women's individual épée
Men's individual sabre
JUDO: Men's half-heavyweight
Women's half-heavyweight
GRECO-ROMAN WRESTLING:
48 kilograms
57 kilograms
68 kilograms
82 kilograms
100 kilograms

JULY 22
WEIGHTLIFTING: 64 kilograms
SHOOTING: Men's 10-meter air rifle
FENCING: Men's individual foil
Women's Individual foil
JUDO: Men's middleweight
Women's middleweight
SWIMMING: Women's 400-meter freestyle
Men's 100-meter freestyle
Women's 100-meter backstroke
Men's 200-meter butterfly
Women's 4x100-meter freestyle relay
GYMNASTICS: Men's team competition

JULY 23
SHOOTING: Men's 50-meter free pistol

At the 1992 Games, Kevin Young won the 400-meter hurdles.

Women's double trap
WEIGHTLIFTING: 70 kilograms
FENCING: Men's team épée
JUDO: Men's half-middleweight
Women's half-middleweight
GRECO-ROMAN WRESTLING:
52 kilograms
62 kilograms
74 kilograms
90 kilograms
130 kilograms

SWIMMING: Men's 400-meter freestyle
Women's 200-meter breaststroke
Men's 100-meter backstroke
Women's 100-meter butterfly
Men's 4x100-meter freestyle relay
GYMNASTICS: Women's team competition

JULY 24
CYCLING: Men's 1-kilometer time trials
SHOOTING: Women's 50-meter standard rifle three positions
Men's double trap
WEIGHTLIFTING: 76 kilograms
EQUESTRIAN: Team three-day event
FENCING: Women's team épée
Men's team sabre
JUDO: Men's lightweight
Women's lightweight
GYMNASTICS: Men's individual all-around
SWIMMING: Men's 200-meter breaststroke
Women's 200-meter individual medley
Men's 100-meter butterfly
Women's 4x100-meter medley relay

JULY 25
CYCLING: Men's individual pursuit
SHOOTING: Men's 50-meter free rifle prone
Men's 25-meter rapid-fire pistol
JUDO: Men's half-lightweight
Women's half-lightweight
FENCING: Women's team foil
Men's team foil
GYMNASTICS: Women's individual all-around
SWIMMING: Women's 800-meter freestyle
Men's 50-meter freestyle
Women's 200-meter backstroke
Men's 200-meter individual medley
Women's 4x200-meter freestyle relay

JULY 26
TRACK AND FIELD: Men's 20-kilometer race walk
Men's shot put
EQUESTRIAN: Individual three-day event
SHOOTING: Women's 25-meter sport pistol
Men's 10-meter running target
WEIGHTLIFTING: 83 kilograms
JUDO: Men's extra-lightweight
Women's extra-lightweight
SWIMMING: Women's 200-meter butterfly
Men's 200-meter backstroke
Women's 50-meter freestyle
Men's 1,500-meter freestyle
Men's 4x100-meter medley relay

JULY 27
ROWING: Men's coxless pair
Women's coxless pair
Men's double sculls
Women's double sculls
Men's coxless four
Women's single sculls
Men's single sculls
KAYAKING: Women's single slalom
CANOEING: Men's single slalom
CYCLING: Women's sprint
Men's team pursuit
SHOOTING: Men's skeet
Men's 50-meter free rifle three positions
WEIGHTLIFTING: 91 kilograms
BEACH VOLLEYBALL: Women's
TRACK AND FIELD: Women's 100 meters
Men's 100 meters
Women's javelin throw
Men's triple jump
DIVING: Women's platform
YACHTING: Men's Finn

JULY 28
TRACK AND FIELD:
Women's marathon
Men's hammer throw
Men's high jump
Women's 5,000 meters
Women's heptathlon
Women's triple jump
ROWING:
Men's lightweight double sculls
Women's lightweight double sculls
Men's lightweight coxless four
Women's quadruple sculls

The U.S. women's relay teams were unstoppable in Barcelona.

Men's quadruple sculls
Women's eight
Men's eight
CANOEING: Men's double slalom
KAYAKING: Men's single slalom
CYCLING: Men's points race
Men's sprint
Women's individual pursuit
Women's points race

Ukraine's Tatiana Goutsu won the all-around gold in 1992.

BEACH VOLLEYBALL: Men's
WEIGHTLIFTING: 99 kilograms
WATER POLO
GYMNASTICS: Men's floor exercise
Women's vault

Men's pommel horse
Women's uneven bars
Men's rings
EQUESTRIAN: Team dressage

JULY 29
TRACK AND FIELD:
Women's 10-kilometer race walk
Women's 400 meters
Men's 400 meters
Men's 110-meter hurdles
Men's 10,000 meters
Women's discus throw
Men's long jump
WEIGHTLIFTING: 108 kilograms
TABLE TENNIS: Women's doubles
YACHTING: Men's IMCO One-Design
Women's IMCO One-Design
Open Star
GYMNASTICS: Men's vault
Women's balance beam
Men's parallel bars
Women's floor exercise
Men's horizontal bar
DIVING: Men's springboard

JULY 30
MODERN PENTATHLON
TABLE TENNIS: Men's doubles
WEIGHTLIFTING: 108-plus kilograms
YACHTING: Open Tornado

Open Laser
Women's Europe
SOFTBALL
MOUNTAIN BIKING:
Men's cross-country
Women's cross-country

JULY 31
CYCLING: Men's road race
BADMINTON: Women's doubles
Men's doubles
ARCHERY: Women's Individual
TABLE TENNIS: Women's singles
FREESTYLE WRESTLING:
48 kilograms
57 kilograms
68 kilograms
82 kilograms
100 kilograms
TRACK AND FIELD:
Men's discus throw
Women's 100-meter hurdles
Women's 400-meter hurdles
Women's 800 meters
Men's 800 meters
DIVING: Women's springboard

AUGUST 1
TRACK AND FIELD:
Women's 800-meter wheelchair
    (non-medal event)
Men's 1,500-meter wheelchair
    (non-medal event)
Women's 200 meters
Men's 200 meters
Men's 400-meter hurdles
Decathlon
BADMINTON: Women's singles
Men's singles
Mixed doubles
YACHTING: Women's 470
Men's 470
Open Soling
ARCHERY: Men's individual
TABLE TENNIS: Men's singles

FIELD HOCKEY: Women's
SOCCER: Women's
EQUESTRIAN: Team jumping

AUGUST 2
TRACK AND FIELD:
Men's 50-kilometer race walk
Men's pole vault
Women's shot put
Women's long jump
Men's 3,000-meter steeplechase
Women's 10,000 meters
DIVING: Men's platform
TENNIS: Women's singles
Men's doubles
ARCHERY:
Women's team
Men's team
RHYTHMIC GYMNASTICS: Group
FREESTYLE WRESTLING:
52 kilograms
62 kilograms
74 kilograms
90 kilograms
130 kilograms
SYNCHRONIZED SWIMMING
FIELD HOCKEY: Men's
BASEBALL

AUGUST 3
CYCLING:
Men's individual time trial
Women's individual time trial
EQUESTRIAN: Individual dressage
KAYAKING:
Men's single 1,000 meters
Women's fours 500 meters
Men's double 1,000 meters
Men's fours 1,000 meters
CANOEING:
Men's single 1,000 meters
Men's double 1,000 meters
TENNIS : Men's singles
Women's doubles
INDOOR VOLLEYBALL: Women's

BOXING:
Light flyweight
Bantamweight
Lightweight
Welterweight
Middleweight
Heavyweight
TEAM HANDBALL: Women's
SOCCER: Men's
TRACK AND FIELD:
Women's high jump
Men's javelin
Women's 4x100-meter relay
Men's 4x100 meter relay
Women's 1,500 meters
Men's 1,500 meters
Men's 5,000 meters
Women's 4x400-meter relay
Men's 4x400-meter relay
BASKETBALL: Men's

AUGUST 4
KAYAKING:
Men's single 500 meters
Women's single 500 meters
Men's double 500 meters
Women's double 500 meters
CANOEING: Men's double 500
    meters
Men's single 500 meters
BASKETBALL: Women's
INDOOR VOLLEYBALL: Men's
BOXING:
Flyweight
Featherweight
Light-welterweight
Light-middleweight
Light-heavyweight
Super-heavyweight
EQUESTRIAN: Individual jumping
RHYTHMIC GYMNASTICS:
Individual
TEAM HANDBALL: Men's
TRACK AND FIELD:
Men's marathon

* Check local listings as some dates may change.

ANSWERS
PUZZLES (pages 92–93)
Olympic Word Spiral
1. Weightlifters; 2. Shot; 3.Torch; 4. Hurdles; 5. Strong; 6. Gold; 7. Dash; 8. Horizontal; 9. Lewis; 10. Swimming; 11. Golf; 12. Fielders; 13. Softball; 14. Lob; 15. Barcelona; 16. Air; 17. Rings; 18. Silver; 19. Ref; 20. Falcons; 21. Shannon; 22. Nets; 23. Steeple; 24. East

Guess Who?
1. Michele Granger; 2. Karch Kiraly; 3. Michael Johnson; 4. Juli Furtado; The letters: EGLOND. The Answer: GOLDEN

The SUM-mer Olympics
$5 + 7 - 2 + 10 + 4 - 11 = 13$

What Do You Know? (page 89)
1. b; 2. Swimming; 3. c; 4. seven; 5. a; 6. b; 7. False; 8. b; 9. Team handball; 10. c; 11. platform; 12. Nadia Comaneci; 13. True.; 14. Muhammad Ali; 15. Softball and soccer; 16. c; 17. c.